WOMAN
You are
WOW

WOMAN
You are
WOW

Fashioned by God's Word
Sculpted in His Love

Mahnykke P. Clark

XULON PRESS

Xulon Press
2301 Lucien Way #415
Maitland, FL 32751
407.339.4217
www.xulonpress.com

Printed in the United States of America.

Paperback ISBN-13: 978-1-63221-205-4
Ebook ISBN-13: 978-1-6322-1206-1

DEDICATION

❧ To my Redeemer and Lord, Jesus Christ. In memory of my mother, the late Carolyn Sims; in remembrance of my sister, DeChanta Alexis Sims; to my dearly loved and awesome aunts, Wilbur Jean Sims, Annie Ruth Thomas and Megan Adams. *To the WOW Women, Pre-Teens, Teens & Toddlers:* Pastoral Leaders, Dr. Gayle Brown, Dr. Darlene Brown, Prophet Kathleen Hawkins, Pastor Marie Roberson and Dr. Lawanna Strowbridge; to my sisters, Heather Hildebrand and Meguill Johnson; to my daughters Darriel Clark, Najee Holmes and Walteara Sims; to my granddaughters, Nyalah Hernandez, Kiara Holmes, Kennedi Ivery, Lyric Holmes and Harper Sink; to my nieces, Brittany Adams, Brittany Allen, Kayla Clark, Kaylen Clark, Felicia Cooper, Keisha Cooper, Krystal Dowdell, Nikaila Dowdell, Nikki Dowdell, Ruby Dowdell, Charyte Hildebrand, Kisten Sims-Hilton, Ashley Johnson, Laila Johnson, Aaliyah Sims and Jada Small; to my cousins, LaRhonda Adams, Roseanne Powell, Betty Sims, Jackie Sims, Joan Sims, and Mitzi Thomas; to my sisters-in-law, Donna Clark, Kaliza Clark, Pastor Monique Clark, Tonya Clark, Angela Sims and Karen Sims; to my god-sister, Andrea Heaven; to Elder Rosalind Belle, Elder Amanda Bethel, Mins. Patricia Roper-Best, Mins. Marette Crawford, Evg. Selina Fairchild, Joan Garrick, Jennie Houston, Ruby

Lewis, Evelyn Ingraham, Princess Ingraham, Paula Larocca, Jackie Moody, Monica Patrick, Evg. Rose Warner, and Dr. Charlotte Byrd-Wilkins.

TABLE OF CONTENTS

Prayer of Salvation

ACKNOWLEDGEMENTS

❧ To the Holy Spirit: Thank You for Your grace, inspiration and revelations in writing this book. Your empowerment was essential to help me triumph against oppositions, which would have prevented me for completing this assignment. Thank You for teaching me to prayer through in faith and declare Your Words of victory and completion!

❧ To Darrell, my husband: I am greatly appreciative to the Lord for the love and dedication you have towards Him. In all my endeavors, you are there cheering, smiling and praying for God's best for me; your support has been astounding. The love and patience you have shown towards me could only be by God's grace. I love you!

❧ Sincere appreciation to Pastor Tawanda Sweeting Anderson, a wow woman indeed. Thank you for your prayers and prophetic words; you were the one who told me that I would write a book for women. Thank you for your integrous stand in Christ and exemplifying a virtuous woman.

❧ Apostle Randy Brown, thank you for your leadership, counsel, and prophetic prayers. I am thankful for the Words of revelation about the necessity of writing this book.

❧ Apostle Tommy Brown, thank you for the many prayers and prophetic words pertaining to God's purpose for my life. Your genuine love for Christ and His Word is an example of continuity and tenacity. Your stance is demonstrative of living faith and declaring the Word of God at all times.

❧ Michelle Cooper: Your genuine friendship is invaluable; your love, encouragement, and compassion are true expressions of godly character. You are an image of what it looks like to walk in God's love and care for others.

❧ Evangelist Teresa Ford: A truth speaker and my sincere, prophetic friend. Thank you for your prayers, the times we have prayed together, and for proclaiming the Word of the Lord so powerfully into my purpose.

❧ Minister Dana Thomas: I am truly grateful for your friendship, prayers, conversations and for sharing your gift of poetic writing. I appreciate the gift of interpreting dreams God has given you, which has brought clarity to what God is saying.

Introduction

ARISE

"Arise from the depression and prostration in which circumstances have kept you – rise to a new life!"
–Isaiah 60:1a, AMPC

UNDESIRABLE CIRCUMSTANCES CAN BECOME distressing and disheartening that can contribute to feelings of insignificance, develop into thoughts and attitudes of defeat, and confessions that do not represent God's grace and victory in your life. Potential and purpose can surrender to dismal, pressuring situations, which can sometimes lead into perplexity and despair.

Even in dim conditions like these, beloved be convinced of Romans 8:28: *"And we know [with great confidence] that God [who is deeply concerned about us] causes all things to work together [as a plan] for good for those who love God, to those who are called according to His plan and purpose"* (AMP). Fiery trials are included in the WOW process and are well fitted into God's plans for you. Your momentary instances of discomfort are molding tools of refinement and your breakthroughs will be used to break barriers in other people's lives.

Be strengthen by God's might and arise; take your upright position in Christ. Defeat is not your destiny, nor is it a description of who you are. Move back the curtains of darkness and allow the victorious Light of Christ to radiate your life. Be stirred! Awake and act; because you will conqueror the circumstances that have immobilized and kept you prostrate.

Your birth is allied with divine purpose; you are created to be powerful and to prevail (Genesis 1:26). Oust obscurity. It is time for you – the authentic you to emerge.

Woman, you are WOW! You are a wonder, greatly admired, outstanding and amazing (Genesis 1:27, 31). WOW declares that you are distinct, necessary and designed for greatness! WOW, in this book, is not a hyperword to stimulate egotism. It is referring to a life submitted and committed to the lordship of Jesus Christ and fulfilling your destiny despite difficult circumstances.

If you think you cannot overcome because of adverse conditions, you will discover that with Christ you can and will move forward and be catapulted beyond where you are and enter into your new and next (Philippians 4:13 AMP). *"Indeed, the former things have come to pass, now I declare new things; before they spring forth I proclaim them to you"* (Isaiah 42:9 AMP), says the Word of the Lord!

Your mind will be transformed, and your faith will be ignited afresh to fulfill God's purposes and plans regardless of life's experiences. Your faith-action and joy will not be circumstantial, but Christ-centered according to His invigorating, infallible Word. *"The Lord will arise upon you, and His glory will be seen upon you"* (Isaiah 60:2 ESV).

Woman You are Wow is a resource of encouragement that will rouse and empower you to arise in adversities, stand and be secure in your true identity, and meet every challenge with the energizing and victorious, notable power of the Holy Spirit.

You are crowned with God's love; so triumph is a part of your spiritual makeup. You are commissioned to conquer and to be the unstoppable you in Jesus Christ (Romans 8:37-39 TPT).

I AM

Fearfully &
Wonderfully Made!

Psalm 139:14

Chapter 1

WITHOUT WALLS

"But Jesus said, Foxes have dens and birds have nests, but I, the Messiah, have no home of my own – no place to lay my head" – Matthew 8:20 TLB

QUESTIONS FLOODED MY MIND: "HOW DID I get here?" "How did it come to this?" "God, tell me why!" "I don't understand!"
The Lord instructed me to resign from my job and move to another location. My past had to be left behind; a severance had to occur. This move would separate me from deceptive influences and help guard me from being enticed back into a precarious relationship God delivered me out of. The Lord had to put miles between me the distractions that were attempting to destroy my life and sabotage my God-purpose. Also, it had been a tough year, and I was exceedingly fatigued! So, a change of address was essential for me to be renewed and restored, to lead me into deeper fellowship with the Lord, and to gain much needed clarity and certainty of His plans for my life.

It is key to know that after the Lord's instruction to move, warfare ensued. Well intentioned people did not agree that I was following God's lead; they prayed that I stay. I literally felt the intensity of their prayers! However, I knew that I had heard from the Lord and that I had to fight for it. Therefore, I resolved that only God's Word would direct the course of my life, and as a result I prayed accordingly. I took an immovable stance to walk in God's will. Without sharing the battle, a prophetess called me and confirmed the Word of the Lord and that no one would alter God's plans for me! God's will is not always easy; yet He gave me a sure Word that would enforce His will.

For a year and a half, things were going exceptionally well in my new location and with the people I lived with; then suddenly it all changed. It began with a difference in demeanor towards me. For instance, I opened the refrigerator, within seconds I heard foot stomps walking towards me. With one hand on the refrigerator to stop me from opening the door, I was demandingly asked, "What do you want?" This happened only twice; but once was enough for me to understand the message loud and clear – hands off. Afterwards, I called a close friend and explained the situation, then asked if she would send me some money so I could purchase food for myself. As we were talking, she said to me, "Don't be surprised if you are asked to leave." Within a week, I was approached and told, "It is time for you to go. I don't know where you are going to go. But you have to go." Where would I go? Where would I live? Who would allow me to stay with them until I could find employment? I did not have a plan; but God did prepare me for the eviction notice. My stay was limited to two and a half months; yet I felt that I was no longer welcomed and decided that I was not going to waste any time departing.

The very next day, I started preparing to leave – within two weeks I vacated the residence.

Fortunately, my daughter allowed me to live with her and her two toddlers. I thought all was well; unexpectantly, things changed quickly. Living there – not even two weeks yet – while we were both in the house, she called me from her cell phone to ask, "How long are you going to be here?" She is a good mother; but at that time, I thought she was going out too much and not spending sufficient quality time with her children. She was displeased that I approached her about this concern; so, she no longer wanted me there. Hurting, with no plan in sight, I told her that I would leave within two weeks or less. The tension was so thick, so tangible, so uncomfortable. My soul was restless; sleep was deficient. I departed her home with nowhere to go – no home to call my own. My Honda Civic became my place of residence. I was devastated, distraught and disgraced – rejection was high on the emotional-Richter scale. While sitting in my car feeling unloved, broken and abandoned, I cried from the innermost depths of my soul unto the Lord.

Without my daughter knowing, the parking lot of the complex where she lived became the place I parked my car nightly – the place I brushed my teeth and slept. Most of the time, I hardly slept because I wanted to remain alert and be sure I was safe; so, I opened my eyes every few seconds. The weight of sleepless nights overtook me, and I just could not remain awake any longer, and decided that I have to trust God and get some sleep. The Lord assured me of His protection through the words of David, *"I lay down and slept. I woke up in safety; for the Lord was watching over me"* (Psalm 3:5). My head dropped from the heaviness of sleep; I could no longer resist and immediately went into an undisturbed, restful sleep. Early in the mornings, I would leave so my presence would not be detected by the occupants of the apartment complex or my daughter.

One afternoon, I was sitting in my car at the public library – a daily hangout. I called a friend just to talk – with the intent of hiding my homeless dilemma. As soon as she answered, a flood of tears began to flow uncontrollably; I revealed to her that I was homeless. She and her husband allowed me to stay with them; and I was incredibly grateful! They welcomed me into their home; and I never felt as though they did not want me there. However, I struggled with thoughts of being an annoyance, and discontented with their daughter having to give up her room for me.

One evening while sitting in my car, feeling depressed, I said, *"Lord, I have no place to lay my head – no place to call my home."* Then, I heard the Holy Spirit say, *"Foxes have holes and birds of the air have nests, but the Son of Man had nowhere to lay His head"* (Luke 9:58). This was not my expected response; however, strength was imparted in my soul. Holy Spirit reminded me that Jesus experienced homelessness and stayed from house to house too. I felt comforted knowing that Jesus could identify with my sufferings (Hebrews 4:15). Reasoning within myself, I decided to leave so this precious family could have their home back – without me constantly being there. Although they never caused me to feel unwanted, I still felt unsettled and in the way.

My next move was with a lady and her daughter. My stay with them was about two weeks. The location made me feel distant and out of sync with the world; I moved again. My feelings were in the driver's seat.

At that time, no one in my family knew that I was living a transient lifestyle. I was too embarrassed and feared being excoriated; still, I decided to call a relative, who lives in another state, and told her that I was homeless. I pleaded with her not tell anyone, especially my father! Of course, my father was the first person she called – lol. He contacted me and made temporary living arrangements for me. While there, I searched for work, went on interviews – nothing. After about 6 months, signs were presented that it was time for me to leave. Without informing me, my bags were already packed, and the sheets and blanket had been removed from the bed I slept in. As soon as I got there that evening, I noticed what had taken place. The message was apparent; so, I turned around and walked out of the house and began sleeping in my car again.

From that point, I was dropped off at a homeless shelter. During that time, I attended a church in Fort Lauderdale, and the Pastor was informed of my predicament; she kindly allowed me to stay temporarily in the church. At night, alone, there I was sleeping on the pulpit's floor. My dad found out where I was staying and made plans for me to live with a relative, who graciously welcomed me in her home. I enjoyed living with her for about 8 months; but sensed the time had come for me to leave. My thoughts were, here I am an adult without any income or provisions; shame hovered over my head. I did find employment; but it was not enough to provide for my needs. I was troubled because my bank account was inadequate, and I did not know how long it would take for me to save money to get my own place. I thought it would be too long for my relative to endure my stay. So, again, I left.

During this homeless period, I was reacquainted with a gentleman that I met about two years prior; we used to converse on a regular basis. I never saw him as anything other than an acquaintance. He was very caring and did whatever he could to help me. He even allowed me to reside in his apartment; he would go and sleep over to his mom's house when it was time to sleep – so our good would not be evil spoken of. Then, it came to the point that he no longer wanted to sleep at his mom's house, but in his own home. I was not comfortable with his decision; nor did I offer any input because it was not my home. He slept in the room; I slept on the sofa.

Although God delivered me from fornication, the Lord sternly warned me not to do it! *"Go, and sin no more!"* The Lord gave us the grace to avoid sexual sin; and we both agreed not to kiss or be sexually intimate. Even when I got dressed, it was always behind closed, locked doors. Although we were not engaging intimately, my soul was still troubled because I wanted to comply with the Word – to be married. I spoke with the gentleman, who had become my fiancé, and told him although we were not engaging in sex, I could no longer live this way; we have to completely obey the Lord. We prepared and were married within that year – about three months later.

I experienced a season of homelessness, shame, rejection, and destitution. How could this be? Why did this happen? Bewildered and broken, I remained committed and close to the Lord. The Lord was not punishing me, nor had He abandoned me (Hebrews 13:5-6 AMPC); God was always present. I was being gracefully broken and fashioned in order to be sent into unfamiliar territories to help build the lives of the broken, and to be sent to people whose homes are the streets.

At the church we attended we were asked to be the leaders of the Outdoor Evangelism Ministry – something I never desired or entered my mind. We led teams into poverty-infested neighborhoods to minister the message of salvation. Alongside my husband, we regularly went street witnessing and shared the Gospel of Jesus Christ with many people who engaged in various walks of life. We used to set up loudspeakers to preach and pray in the church's parking lot; people could hear us blocks away. The preaching traveled the airwaves to crack, prostitution, alcohol and gambling houses. Some people would sit outside in their lawn chairs, blocks away, to hear God's Word. People who drove by would join us to receive prayer and hear the Message. Regardless of what lifestyles they were practicing, we prayed for them and treated them with love and respect. During New Year's Eve services, my husband would go out in the streets, gather and invite many drug dealers and their associates to church, and they came. Inside, the evangelism team would be ready and waiting to minister and pray with them.

I grew up in a well-to-do environment and did not know much about the streets. The destitution and homelessness that I experienced allowed me to be able to identify with and have compassion for the people God was calling me to. This process of humility and equipping was necessary preparation for effectiveness. I exited that season with a home, a husband, promotion, new relationships, new spiritual experiences, and a stronger relationship with the Lord.

I did not like what I had gone through; I told the Lord that I did not like it. He revealed to me that Jesus had to complete His experiences before He could become the Author and Finisher of our faith. So, before I could do what He was calling me to do, I had to complete my experiences too. *"Although He was a Son, He learned [active, special] obedience through what He suffered. And, [His completed experience] making Him perfectly [equipped], He became the Author and Source of eternal salvation to all those who give heed and obey Him* (Hebrews 5:7-9 AMPC; 12:2-3 AMPC).

I could have allowed this experience to influence me to become resentful towards God and turn away from Him – thinking that He withdrew His love from me and does not care. There were times when I could not *see* my way; when God's *voice* seemed silent; when I did not *know* what God was doing, and when I could not *feel* His Presence (Job 23:10 AMPC). In spite of all of this, I had an inward knowing that God is not an absent Father; that He is faithful and will not leave me in this situation. Also, I knew that God already had an exit plan – that this too will pass. Satan will always offer another way out, which seems easier and less painful. But, if I had decided to implement a deliverance plan by getting involved with a sugar daddy for monetary gain, my bills may have been paid, and other financial needs met, but it would have come with a high price – my soul and a violation in my relationship with the Lord. Many like to say, "God understands." Yes, He does; yet God will not violate His Word for anyone. He will justify the repentant person through the atonement of His Son, but never validate sin or tell us it is alright (Hebrews 2:16-17 AMPC).

By spending treasured time reading and studying God's Word, we become more acquainted with His character and ways, and discover that He will never discredit Himself (Hebrews 6:16-19). Being homeless was certainly not a part of my plans for prosperity; but God used it to prepare me for His plans. God's plans for our lives are always to prosper us – not perish (Jeremiah 29:11). God's prosperity is not always about money, although this can be included, it is more about flourishing as the person God created you to be by living life according to His Word.

What God calls us to fulfill in our lives, He may not always reveal the process. However, you can be certain that He will shepherd you through it all. *"Who shall ever separate us from Christ's love? Shall suffering and affliction and tribulation? Or calamity and distress? Or persecution or hunger or destitution or peril or sword"* (Romans 8:35 AMPC)? Yet in all these things, God's love for me remained entrenched in my heart, and there was an engrained knowing that the Father was watching over me, and that restoration would come (Romans 8:37).

I did not have any foresight before I went through the experiences of homelessness; nor was I forewarned or given a personal prophecy. However, when it happened, I held on to: the written Word which reveal God's attributes; the rhema which steadied me; prayer which strengthened me, and Holy Spirit led worship that ushered me into His Presence where the fullness of joy dwells, which shook and lifted the clutches of depression.

During trials, our love walk will be tested. There were people who gossiped about me when I was homeless, and God revealed some of them to me. Yet, God gave me the grace to walk in His love and forgiveness towards them and treat them as though nothing was ever said. God used many people to lend a helping hand during my season of homelessness; consequently, I am genuinely thankful to each person and family who welcomed me to live in their home!

What the enemy meant for my demise and to cause division; it did not work! God used this for His glory and for our good. The refining process was not for me only; it was also for some of them. These experiences are shared for the purpose of *mapping* my homeless journey – not to bring an indictment – and to emphasize that with God, we are victorious and are always at home with Him!

Chapter 2

AUTHENTIC BEAUTY

"I thank you because I am awesomely made, wonderfully; your works are wonders – I know this very well." – Psalm 139:14 CJSB

YES, YOU ARE DISTINCT, SET APART AND MARKED for God's purpose; you are a resemblance of the Creator. You are astonishing; Woman you are Wow! Wow is a word used to express wonder, amazement, great pleasure, outstanding success or great admiration. All of God's creations have worth, value and purpose. You are beautiful and beloved; God is in absolute awe of you; marvelous are the works of the Creator's hands. Wow describes you!

Beauty is not defined by specific measurements of your hips, lips, thighs and breast. Nor is it defined by your particular nationality or your name. This kind of beauty is not described by whether your hair is long or short; coarse or soft; brown, black, red or blonde. Neither does it have anything to do with your complexion – light, medium or dark. It is not dependent upon age, financial wealth, educational status or social surveys. This beauty is not a work of your own hands but realizing that you are a display of the marvelous workmanship of God. Woman, you are a wonder of God's workmanship – a breathtaking master-piece of the Creator.

You are beautiful regardless of the specifics because God created you with authentic beauty and with a uniqueness that is solely you. Your origin is undeniable; and you are not a reproduction of someone else; you are exclusively you. Embrace your beautiful!

The Kadupul Flower (blooms only at night) and Juliet Rose are rated some of the most valuable flowers because of their beauty, rarity and difficulty to cultivate. A common process is that these flowers grow in dirt, an essential filthy substance, yet yield the most valuable and beautiful flowers.

Difficulties have their benefits. God uses these times to shape our character, remove weed attitudes, deepen our trust in Him and grow us gracefully. We all share in our portion of problems – no one is exempt. Through the hardships we experience, it can produce a new awareness of ourselves and a fresh revelation of God. During difficulties, our thoughts can teeter between whether to faint or to be rigidly fixed in faith; our faith feels stretched beyond what we sometimes think we cannot bear. Endurance is a nec-essary attribute because without it, we will surrender our faith and forfeit our future (2 Corinthians 4:16-17). It is effortless to quit; but requires effort to endure and a men-tality of persistence when the pressure is on. Everything we go through has the capacity to yield a righteous harvest and glorify the Lord in the beauty of holiness.

Satan can be adamant about attacking our identity in times of crisis – contributing to self-blame, rejection, defeat and shame. Some things we go through can be no fault of our own; yet, he will try to deceive us so we can falsely point the finger at ourselves. Occasionally, he will use people to say negative words that can weigh heavily on our minds, question our worth and be critical and harsh towards who we are and why we are not like someone else. These kinds of comments can also lead to pondering whether something is wrong with us – defective.

Many years ago, several of my family members were discussing complexion. One of my uncle's turned and looked directly in my face and said, "What happened to you?" I assumed he thought he was advantaged because he was lighter complexioned, and I was disadvantaged. Another relative said to me that a particular cousin looked better than me. A former associate of our family said that one of my sisters looked better than me. A cousin said to me, "Oh, I see; it is just your face that is darker." I was valedictorian at South FL Bible College; and someone I invited said, "I did not know you had it in you." I have been told that I do not look like an author; but, I am. I have been told that I do not look like a minister; but, I am. What does an author, minister or valedictorian look like? As I was thinking on these things, the Lord guided me to His Word. *"For man looks at the outward appearance, but the Lord looks at the heart"* (1 Samuel 16:7b). People will judge you by how you look and what you do or do not look like. I was one of several speakers at a women's clergy event; afterwards, a lady said that when she looked at me, she assumed I had nothing – little or no anointing. Her opinion completely changed after I ministered the Word of God.

Be confident and comfortable in who you are in Christ; resist using your efforts to validate yourself for the sake of people. You are who God says you are, whether they agree or not. Allow no misjudging words to move you or change your view on how God made you. It does not matter if your personality type is sanguine, choleric or melancholic; God uses them all according to His will. What does matter is that you are an authentic beauty who is clothed and filled with God's purpose, power and presence. Jesus did not look like the Bread of Life (John 6:35-36; 41-42), nor did the scribes believe that Jesus is God (Mark 2:5-7); Paul did not look like a bold apostle (2 Corinthians 10:7, 11); David did not look like he was chosen to be king (1 Samuel 16:7). What people negatively thought of them did not stop them from being who they were nor did it prevent them from accomplishing God's purposes. They knew and understood that their missions came from the Lord.

Intentionally, words are sometimes used to depreciate a person's value and acceptance. Oppositely, words can positively build up and reinforce your necessity and worth! Choose which words you will believe and apply. Irrespective of who they are, reject the debilitating, demeaning, derogatory names or words that people categorized you as! No, that is not you! Sticks and stones may not have broken your bones; instead, cunning, cutting words can be used to hurt and break you. For others, your bones may have actually been broken through physical abuse. Some have been battered to the point of despising their existence and questioning their value. Receive this fact: You are an intentional being and are meant to be here. God decided your birth! So, your true value and existence originates from Him. All of God's creations have His divine imprint; and He never created anyone or anything that does not possess worth and purpose. You were fashioned in the likeness and image of God (Genesis 1:27); when God created you, He created you in His divine love and acceptance. He called you very good! Sometimes determinations of our value and reception are based on people's estimations. For many, social media has become a tool to measure acceptance. Value and acceptance are not derived from social media likes and hearts nor does it originate from the number of times your images and comments are shared. People's opinions change like the turning of pages in a book. But there is one Book whose comments about you that are concrete and consistent – the Bible.

Comparing yourself and being people-opinion focused (2 Corinthians 10:12) can generate wrong self-thoughts and perceptions about God's love and approval; love and acceptance gives a sense of having worth, being wanted and welcomed. Love and acceptance can make one feel included or a part of a whole; it gives the sense that we matter, and we are supposed to be here. God's love is demonstrative, and Jesus went through great, excruciating experiences to prove it. Demonstrative is characterized by open exhibition, serving to prove the truth of anything; it is unquestionable, certain, evident, convincing and conclusive.

God is love; love is a conquering spirit. *"Yet even in the midst of all these things, we triumph over them all, for God has made us to be more than conquerors, and his demonstrated love is our glorious victory in everything!"* (Romans 8:37 TPT). Nothing in life or any of our experiences can modify God's unconditional, victorious love for us. Here is indisputable evidence: 1} *"For God loved the world so much that he gave his one and only Son, so that everyone who believes in him will not perish but have eternal life"* (John 3:16 NLT). 2} *"But God clearly shows and proves His own love for us, by the fact that while we were still sinners; Christ died for us"* (Romans 5:8 AMP). 3} *"His example is this: Because his heart was focused on the joy of knowing that you would be his, he endured the agony of the cross and conquered its humiliation, and now sits exalted at the right hand of the throne of God!"* (Hebrews 12:2b TPT).

In spite of what people say or think, you are who God says you are. Satan will use people close to you to launch personal attacks against your identity and worth; but do not allow their words to control the narratives on any of the pages of your life's story. And, certainly do not repeat their words or declare destructive things about yourself. Ask God for His grace not internalize and agree with their comments. Love them; but reject their remarks. Do not permit those moments to become your mindset. Woman, you are authentically beautiful! You are an expression of the love and spectacular genius of God. Embrace your authentic beauty. Embrace how God created you – exceptionally!

Supremely Exquisite Workmanship

"For we are His workmanship [His own master work, a work of art], created in Christ Jesus" (Ephesians 2:10a). God, the Master Designer, created the universe (Psalm 19:1) and He created you. Did you know that your physical birth is wonderful gift from the Lord (Psalm 127:3; 139:13-16)? Celebrate the heavenly Architect; you are one of a kind. No one else has your divine design. However, there is a different, a more glorious, workmanship that Paul is referring to.

Ladies at times we desire to have a makeover; so, we go shopping to make this happen, which can include buying new makeup, clothes, jewelry and accessories. A new hairstyle and hair color often accompany the look we are desiring because we want to look beautiful and feel different – even be different. Although these things can give us a new external look, what it cannot do is give us a new heart and cause us to be internally different. This requires an inner makeover by the Divine Artisan, Holy Spirit. In your first birth, you did not have any say in the matter; however, in this birth you do. You decide whether you want this internal makeover by responding to God's Message of love and eternity, the Gospel of Jesus Christ.

We dress for success to present ourselves as images of qualified candidates and to obtain a new position or promotion believing that our outward clothing points to inward success. This dress code is commonly necessary, but temporal and material. God has a new set of clothes that He wants to give to those who do not personally know Him. He desires to give you an eternal makeover and wants to clothe you with Himself – His quality of life and success. Jesus said, *"Do not be surprised that I have told you, you must be born again [reborn from above – spiritually transformed, renewed, sanctified]"* (John 3:7 AMP). Holy Spirit's makeover transforms your entire being and existence; your nature becomes new and your garments (character) too. Only through repentance of sins and real faith in Jesus Christ as your Lord and Savior can this rebirth happen. There is absolutely no other way to be clothe in Christ.

"Therefore, if anyone is in Christ, he is a new creation; old things have passed away; behold, all things have become new" (2 Corinthians 5:17 NKJV). The old, previous moral spiritual condition has passed away; new things have come – a spiritual awakening has occurred. You have become a new creation – a new workmanship of the Lord. A revelation of

your new and true identity is revealed; a new order of life has come lead by a new Master (Christ); you are no longer ruled by the power of sin and Satan; you have direct and intimate communication with the Creator of life; your perspective on life is new; your life is governed by the truth of God's Word; your will and ways become new; God becomes primary and precious in your life; you are forgiven of your sins; the Spirit comes and lives inside you with victorious power to live for Christ and overcome obstacles. You have become a brand-new creation in Christ Jesus – not renovated, refurbished or reformed – but a brand-new stunning you – a more superior workmanship of God.

You may think that things are well in your life and you do not need Christ because you are already successful and have gained financial wealth and people-popularity. You may even be a social media sensation. Is your soul more valuable than the amount of money in your bank account? Is your worth and identity determined by your financial assets and accomplishments? *"For what use is it to gain all the wealth and power of this world, with everything it could offer you, at the cost of your own life? And what could be more valuable to you than your own soul?* (Mark 8:36-37 TPT). Sadly, media has informed us of people who were millionaires; yet felt hopeless, and committed suicide. They had all the wealth, but were soul-rupt (empty), depressed and void of true life. The wealth of this world is impermanent; your soul will abide permanently in eternity – heaven or hell. No amount of money or success by the world's standards will have any impact on your eternal dwelling place – only your rebirth. Popularity with people carries no weight in God's kingdom – only Christ. You do not have to choose one or the other; you can have both Christ and wealth. Here is the caveat: *"If riches increase set not your heart on them* (Psalm 62:10 AMP). God blesses many of His people with monetary prosperity; however, materialism is not to become the center of affection and guide for life. If it does, it has become a snare and a god. Nothing and no one are to be prioritized before the Lord God. Even if you may not be financially wealthy, you are wealthy in Christ Jesus; and He will meet every one of your needs according to His riches in glory in Christ Jesus (Philippians 4:19), because godly wealth and good success comes for above (Joshua 1:8; Psalm 75:6-7).

In lack, we seek God steadfastly until the breakthrough. When the money comes, be sure to continue in prayer and not fall into the temptation of prayerlessness or praying less because God has provided the need. In other words, because you have been relieved of the financial stress, do not release the priority of prayer nor loosen your relationship with the Lord.

Spiritual regeneration, the second birth – the real you – is the greatest, most indispensable gift from the Lord. It is a supreme makeover that never fades and transforms you from the inside-out, sculpting you into an exquisite workmanship of Divine artistry.

This birth draws you to your heavenly Father, the One who you are meant to pattern your life after. Your authenticity comes from the Creator and you have the awesome responsibility to represent Him, here in the earth being authentically you!

Chapter 3

WORTHY CONFRONTATION

*"They stood her in plain sight of everyone and said,
"Teacher, this woman was caught red-handed in
the act of adultery." – John 8:3-4 MSG*

W HAT TEMPTED THIS WOMAN TO COMMIT
marital infidelity? Was she longing for affection and appreciation – being wanted and
loved? Was it a forced act or did she just enjoy being pro-
miscuous? Was she searching for fulfillment? Was it a
season in her life where she thought this was the only way
she could provide for herself? The Scriptures are silent as
to her reason. Caught in the act, afraid and void of hope
because she likely knew the penalty of her actions. It is
eye-opening to know that whether someone is caught in
an immoral act or not, it is impossible to hide from God.
Secret acts cloaked in darkness are visible in God's sight
(Psalm 139:12). Regardless of her reasons for indulging in
an unlawful relationship, an unexpected divine encounter
was about to happen. She would soon meet the Man Who

will give her beauty for ashes – a new heart, a new perspective and a new beginning.

All eyes were on her as she was made to stand in the midst of the crowd. I can imagine people sneering, shaking their heads and unleashing excoriating remarks with soul-piercing facial expressions to back it up. She was publicly embarrassed, exposed and thought her execution was sure (Leviticus 20:10; Deuteronomy 22:22-24).

To the heartless and calculating Pharisees and scribes, the adulteress was viewed as a nobody – a worthless object to bait and trap Jesus – her life did not matter to them. They were more concerned about Jesus offending the Mosaic Law than the redeeming restoration of this woman.

The scribes and Pharisees specified, *"Now in the Law Moses commanded us to stone such a woman [to death]. So, what do You say [to do with her – what is Your sentence* (John 8:5)*]?"* Jesus knowing their motives declared, *"He who is without [any] sin among you, let him be the first to throw a stone"* (John 8:7). Being conscious-stricken with Truth, her accusers left one-by-one. They were stone struck with a convicting question of introspection. No one could raise a hand to cast a stone at her. Jesus said, *"Woman where are your accusers? Has no man condemned you?* (John 8:10).

Alone, standing in the center court was Jesus and the adulteress; this is a great place to be! This is exactly the place where Jesus wanted the adulteress – talking with Him one-on-one, face-to-face with the transforming Word (John 1:1). This Man Jesus was different from all of the other men she had been with or ever known. She was caught by cold-hearted critics; but was captured by the convicting and compassionate Jesus. He stepped into the situation and interceded to save this woman's life. For the first time, she had a real revelation of her worth and value because she humbly stood before and listened to the One – the Originator of her worth and value.

At times, it may have seemed as though everyone walked out on you and no one was around to affirm, uphold, encourage, defend or support you. Jesus will not walk out on you; summons Him. He will come alongside you through the hard times and in His tender mercies give you His healing counsel and comfort (2 Corinthians 1:4 MSG).

For change to occur in our lives, we have to be confronted by the confrontational and caring Jesus; this is a worthy and necessary conversation that must happen. Some confrontations are for you and God alone – not the crowd. You are God's worth-manship; knowing and understanding your worth is a valuable reinforcer that acts as a helmet to safeguard your mind from satanic lies. God sent His Son to pay the highest price necessary to redeem, restore and reconcile you to Himself (John 3:16). *"Go and sin no more,"* Jesus declared (John 8:11). Grace will highlight areas in our lives that require change. The intent is not to embarrass, but to empower us to walk in a new way – holiness (Ephesians 1:4 CJSB). Love covers sin (1 Peter 4:8), yet it uncovers it too; it is a concealer and revealer. God will reveal your sin to lead you into repentance and reconciliation and to draw you into the intimate place of the Most High God, not make you a public spectacle as the religious leaders did to the adulterous woman. God will never justify sin, but He will justify the offender who turns away from sin and turns to Him through repentance. *"For with the heart a person believes [in Christ as Savior] resulting in his justification [that is, being made righteous – being freed of the guilt of sin and made acceptable to God]; and with the mouth he acknowledges and confesses [his faith openly], resulting in and confirming [his] salvation* (Romans 10:10 AMP).

In today's culture, it is the norm to have sex in dating (1 Corinthians 6:18); it is the norm to have multiple sexual partners (Galatians 5:19); it is the norm to be uncommitted to each other. It is the norm to claim someone else's husband as your man or vice versa (Matthew 5:27). We are living in a world that glorifies nudity and is intoxicated with sexual immorality. There is a deceptive freedom in fornication – giving the illusion that it is a way of fulfillment and happiness. Listen, fornication is not the solution for acceptance. Fornication (*porneia*), is a broad word that includes all kinds and forms of sexual immorality and acts whether married or unmarried. Even though a majority of the population is engaging in premarital sex, God never has and never will endorse it. Fornication does not make you fabulous nor is it like choosing and keeping up with the latest fashions. Sexual intercourse is so much deeper. Choosing fornication with one partner or multiple ones affects your spirit, mind and emotions; it has emotional, physical, spiritual and eternal repercussions (1 Corinthians 6:9, 12-20).

At age 21, I was pregnant with my second child – out of wedlock. Three years later, I had my third child outside of marriage also. I experienced regret for my choice of choosing their father; I felt that I failed them as their mom because he was an absent father for most of their lives. Our relationship was largely built on satisfying fleshly desires (lust). I dated him mainly because of his looks, complexion and physic; he was also appealing because of the type of job he had. I did not consider his character until after I became a single mother; my perspective about him changed and my life too. No longer was I the center of attention; two beautiful babies had to be cared for.

Both my daughters, also rebellious, became pregnant at age 16. They also experienced fatherlessness with their children, periodically not receiving financial and emotional support.

Their father's broken promises to spend quality time with our children was heart breaking. It is very painful for a mother to raise her child with the absence of the father as well as trying to cope with rejection of their child, as well as their own. When a mother's child is rejected, mom feels the rejection too.

Denial of paternity is often an issue – mom on one side, potential father on the other. The breach of certainty due to promiscuity, with an innocent child or children caught in the middle of conflict, has often concluded with the mother not knowing the identity of the father. Consequently, an innocent child often contends with thoughts and feelings of abandonment and insecurity – sobbing because of not knowing who their dad is or because of his lack of love and involvement in their life.

Mom do not get caught up in the world's culture. Teach your daughters – sons too – in the way they should go; point them in the right direction (Proverbs 22:6). Steer them away from pre-marital sex (1 Corinthians 6:18; 1 Thessalonians 5:22); explain to them that they are worth waiting on their God-approved spouse.

It is wise to remove yourself from people and environments that lure you into sin. Here is clear counsel, *"Enter not into the path of the wicked, and go not in the way of evil men. Avoid it, do not go on it; turn from it and pass on* (Proverbs 4:14-15 AMPC). Paul exhorts us to flee fornication; run for your life! Take flight and do not give any weight to ungodly opinions. Mark those who cause a divide or hinder you from obeying the Truth of God's Word. Some people care about gratifying their sexual desire with you, but care nothing about your salvation and wellbeing. A common manipulative method Satan uses towards Christian girls and women is by attacking and causing you to question your beliefs (Genesis 3:3). He wants you to let your guard down and succumb to giving your body to someone that is not your husband.

Ladies, teens, God did not create our bodies for sexual immorality; some freedoms are satanic tools of enslavement (1 Corinthians 6:13-17). Jesus cares about every aspect of your life. He gave a guide – the Bible – for your safety and wellbeing. Yes, God's Word is ancient, but it is not outdated. His Word is eternal and was written for all times and all ages. His Word still applies today! *"What you say goes, God, and stays, as permanent as the heavens. Your truth never goes out of fashion, it's up-to-date as the earth when the sun comes up"* (Psalm 119:89 MSG).

Even if you have fallen into the pit of promiscuity, there is help, hope and healing. The cycle of sexual sin can be broken right now! Your deliverance is one decision away from being a reality. You cannot close your eyes and hope the fleshly cravings will go away. No, the caring confrontation with Christ is compulsory. It is an unavoidable meeting of worth, intimacy, liberty, regeneration and eternity. Jesus died a sacrificial death to prove you have value and to exhibit His unconditional love for you.

Just as the woman caught in adultery, declare this day you will no longer be caught in sexual snares and intertwined in immoral relationships. Interlock with Jesus; allow the Holy Spirit to develop within you a spirit of self-control. He will strengthen you and give you the grace to say "NO" to temptation, regardless of how it feels or how magnetic the attraction. Saying "YES" to God will lead you to face Him and experience His life empowering Presence.

Go, Get Your Husband

"At this, Jesus said to her, Go, call your husband and come back here." – John 4:16

As Jesus was resting at the well, a Samaritan woman approached to draw water. Jesus initiated a conversation with her by asking her to give Him a drink. Jesus was naturally thirsty; yet, it was also an opportune time for Him to address barriers in her life. Their conversation opened the way for revelation and rescue.

The Jews of that day considered Samaritans to be permanently unclean and preferred not to associate with them. Based on religious and cultural expectations, she was surprised that Jesus would talk with her being that she was a Samaritan, a woman, a harlot, and drink from a vessel that belonged to her! This was frowned upon! But she was exactly who Jesus wanted and the kind of person who Jesus sought for – the outcasts. Jesus, a Jew, did not allow customary bias, race, ethnicity, gender or her current involvement in fornication and cohabitation forbid Him from associating with her. Matter of fact, Jesus was in the right place at the right time to have a worthy confrontation. He did not travel aimlessly; every place He went had divine purpose and a Kingdom agenda attached. This encounter was intentional, and the conversation was mapped to lead her to a specific place of realization and fulfilment (John 4). Their discussion took a sharp u-turn that suddenly compelled her to confront the insufficiency and immorality in her life. *"At this, Jesus said, "Go, call your husband and come back. The woman answered, "I do not have a husband." Jesus said to her, "You have correctly said, 'I do not have a husband'; for you have had five husbands, and the man you are now living with is not your husband. You have said this truthfully"* (John 4:16-18 AMP). Truth confronts to challenge what you are conformed to. Where does your influence derive? What you believe will be a director of your decisions and how you live life. The Lord does not sanction cohabitation (shacking). People make comments such as: "God does not mind us living with each other or getting to know each other – referring to sex – to find out if we should marry." Another remark is: "We humbled ourselves and made our vows to God; we just have to obey *man's* part – making light of obeying the laws of the land, which God said to obey (Romans 13:1-2). These comments point to a lack of knowledge and understanding of God's Word or reasoning to justify immoral behavior. When you face Christ, you face Truth. In God's Presence, He is revealed, and you are too. Your spiritual senses awaken and your need for Him becomes obvious.

The main reason for this convergence was communion with Christ and conversion – to reveal and fill a thirst that only Jesus could provide. The Word, in the flesh, had a personal encounter with this spiritually vacant woman (John 1:14). At times people entertain multiple partners trying to satisfy an emptiness they sometimes cannot explain or are not sure what it is they need. It is not what they need, it is who they need – Jesus.

The Samaritan woman thought Jesus was speaking about natural water to please her natural thirst. Just as natural thirst indicates a need to be replenished with water, the soul has a capacity and need for spiritual water – the Holy Spirit and God's Word. Thirst is also a signal of dehydration because of not drinking enough fluids; likewise, when your spirit is void of God, dissatisfaction and desiccation is present.

Make the choice to no longer drink from the cesspool of fornication. Jesus said, *"If anyone is thirsty, let him come to Me and drink. He who believes in Me, as the Scripture said, 'From his innermost being will flow rivers of living water'"* (John 7:37-38).

The Samaritan woman entered into Jesus' presence as an adulteress; but exited with new perspective on life, new hope and new revelation of her worth and purpose that was founded in God's love, grace and forgiveness. She went to the well to draw water; but Jesus was at the well to draw her to Him.

Jesus invites you to be redeemed, replenished, and revitalized through a vital connection with Him. The Savior, the Holy Spirit baptizer, calls the thirsty soul to come to Him and drink; He is the only one that can quench your parched soul and spirit and cause you to experience true fulfillment, peace, joy and eternal life. Jesus invites you to restart – began again – by having a worthy confrontation with Him that will change your entire life, redirect your course, and continually grant you to drink from the life-giving well of the Holy Spirit. Take in, ingest, be immersed in and consumed by the Spirit of God, who will embrace and esteem you like no one else can – man or woman. He will empower you to go and sin no more and become a transformed temple of the Spirt of God (1 Corinthians 6:12-20 MSG).

You may have been called all kinds of belittling names to depreciate your worth and treated as an outcast – even from family. You may have been the topic of gossip. It may appear as though no one cares, or is concerned about the pains of self-disappointment, and silent frustrations that constantly batter your soul. Jesus knows and cares; He feels what you feel. *"For we do not have a High Priest who is unable to sympathize and understand our weaknesses and temptations, but One who has been tempted [knowing exactly how it feels to be human] in every respect as we are, yet without [committing any] sin"* (Hebrews 4:15 AMP). Jesus, *"heals the brokenhearted and binds up their wounds [healing their pain and comforting their sorrow]"* (Psalm 147:3).

Sometimes, people like to remind you of your past mistakes to humiliate you or use them to measure your worth and value to society or emit condemnation. Dismiss their remarks; decide to leave your past behind (Philippians 3:13-14); and do not bind yourself to your slip-ups any longer. Jesus' blood and forgiveness have the power to cleanse and reach you in the lowest of valleys, lift you up, and take you out. There is nothing you have done that has the capacity to continue to hold you captive when Christ becomes your Redeemer. He said, *"I, even I, and He who blots out and cancels your transgressions, for My own sake, and I will not remember your sins"* (Isaiah 43:25). Jesus' redemptive work paid sin's debt, canceled the charge and completely erased it. The Lord does not keep record and you should not either. Even your past experiences will serve as instruments to draw others to Christ.

The only way to receive this gift of great grace is by having that upfront, up-close worthy confrontation and surrendering your life to Him. You do not have to wait any longer (John 4:26). You are always welcomed to the well of Life, Jesus Christ, because in His eyes you are worth it! Hear God's love in this Scripture *"For you will bring me continual revelation of resurrection life, the path to the bliss that brings me face-to-face with you"* (Psalm 16:11 TPT).

Chapter 4

FRAGRANT BEAUTY

"Through our yielded lives he spreads the fragrance of the knowledge of God everywhere we go. We have become the unmistakable aroma of the victory of the Anointed One." – 2 Corinthians 2:14b-15 TPT

PERFUME IS ONE OF MY FAVORITE ACCESSORIES. Have you ever thought about why you wear perfume? I enjoy smelling pretty and people commenting on its pleasant scent. Also, there is an individuality that can be exhibited through fragrance. Scented oils can affect a women's emotions by applying those dabs of perfume that somehow finishes her look and boosts her happiness. Fragrance is more than a smell; it is also strongly associated with memory. For instance, you may smell the aroma of sweet potatoes in a bakery and it may remind you of your mom's delicious sweet potato pie and the cherished family meals, especially during the holidays. Similarly, the sense of smell can alert you to dangerous scents such as fire or gas. After a strenuous workout, an unpleasant scent means a bath is needed. Essential oils are used in aromatherapy to promote relaxation and to relieve stress. Smell can determine if you will eat or not; if it smells spoiled, it will not be eaten. Scent is a deciding factor as to whether to purchase a specific perfume; smell is a significant sense that is beneficial to everyday life.

Esther was a woman who was well acquainted with oils and perfumes. And, so were the other young virgin women who went through the beauty treatment process for a chance to obtain favor from King Ahasuerus (Esther 2:12-13). For twelve months they were daily saturated in oils and perfumes for perhaps only one night with the king. If she did not have special favor with the king, the maiden went to the second harem reserved for the king's concubines (2 Samuel 20:3). She never went to the king again, unless summoned by name or the king delighted in her (Esther 2:14).

I imagine the loneliness and absence of real love, children and family that many of those young women may have experienced. *"Let beautiful young virgins be sought for the king; and let the king appoint officers in all the provinces of his kingdom, that they may gather all the beautiful young virgins"* (Esther 2:2-3). *"Esther was brought also to the king* (Esther 2:8c). These women were taken from their parents, homes and families. Their desires or choices did not matter; they had to go whether they wanted to or not. Some of those women probably felt like objects of abuse rather than persons with real value or privileged. Before going into the king's bed chambers, they were allowed to take with them whatever they desired such as jewels and apparel to please the king (Esther 2:13). According to the historian Josephus there were 400 virgins (The Complete Works of Josephus, p. 238). Imagine the competition and concern and possibly wondering if they were beautiful enough, dressed eloquent enough to be chosen queen.

Before Jesus became my Lord and Savior, I dated a guy who I deeply loved; I was all in and fully committed. I discovered a few years later that his commitment was not mutual and that I was just one of the many women he dated. When I spoke with him about the matter, he always had a clever way of downplaying things – and it worked. Nothing was ever a big deal to him. Naïve and ignorant, I continued to date him, gave him money at times, and always dressed and smelled in a manner to capture and keep his attention. I used to internally compare myself with the other women contemplating whether I was prettier and more physically attractive. Eventually, he said I was his number one woman and those other women meant nothing to him. Feelings of fear, uncertainty and uneasiness became a part of my daily emotions. At times, an entire weekend would pass without hearing from him; and I knew he was with another woman. I called; he would not answer. Anxiously waiting to hear his voice, I used to sit by the phone peering at it – hoping it would ring, hoping it was him. I was a part of an assembly line of women waiting for my turn to be with him.

The *ungodly* soul ties were tightly woven and thick. Soul ties are deeply rooted invisible bonds that can have strong grips on your emotions and mind, and can feel like you are being sucked in by a power that seems irresistible. It is a magnetic connection between people who have been physically intimate with each other. Soul ties can also form by having consistent, personal conversations, in which you intimately share your heart. Soul ties are so solid because they are physical and spiritual; they are soul-binding ties. Sex is a joining force that glues people together (1 Corinthians 6:12-20; 1 Thessalonians 5:23).

I was pregnant with his first child – from someone who made it clear to me that he did not want children. Three years later, I had another baby from the same man who continued to fulfil his words of not wanting children. My entire life changed; his life continued as a casanova – a ladies' man. How was I ever going to leave him alone? I loved him and birthed two of his children. Daily my soul ached, longing to be with him and desiring that he would want to be with me too. The scents I wore were labeled *Worthless*, *Rejection*, *Wanting and Fearful.*

One day, my mother said to me, "Please, don't go back to him." She knew my heart was broken. It was something about those six words my Mom spoke that sparked a will in me to leave him alone even in the midst of excruciating emotional pain, and simultaneously dealing with his lack of involvement in our girl's lives. The decision was made; I walked away from him. Wounded and wanting to be with him, I remained determined to fulfill the words of my Mother.

Physically, I no longer associated with him; however, my mind and emotions were still tied and knotted to him; because, the next person I dated had to have a similar dark complexion, facial and bodily features like my children's father. I assumed that another man who looked like him would help me completely get over him – wrong assumption. I still wanted to be with my children's father; substitution was not the answer.

I did not think it was possible; I thought that the agony of not being with him would be forever settled in my heart. How was the scent of his presence ever going to be purified from my soul? Who could untie me and loose me from this attraction – this strong captivity? Smiling, functioning, living, yet real life and joy were absent. Some years later, I was taken captive by another; this time He was the right One. *"But thank God! He has made us his captives and continues to lead us along in Christ's triumphal procession"* (2 Corinthians 2:14 NLT). This captivity is different; it is filled with limitless dimensions of God's unfailing and liberating love. Being captured and led by Christ will always lead to triumphant joy and freedom.

"Through our yielded lives he spreads the fragrance of the knowledge of God everywhere we go" (2 Corinthians 2:14b-15 TPT). I yielded to the Man who can heal all hurts and failed expectations regardless of how deep and how long. Christ is the soul-tie Breaker and the Healer of broken hearts (Psalm 147:3)! The fragrances of my life began to change through my devotion to Christ and learning about Him – more than an intellectual or surface knowledge, but a heart knowledge that transformed by mind and ways. When Christ becomes the Savior and Captain of our lives, we become an aroma of victory of the Anointed One. Our lives become inspired by the Holy Spirit that emits the fragrance of Christ. The same breath, life-force (*pneuma*) that created the universe and continues to sustain it, will sustain you and enable you to conquer.

Do not sit in sorrow and allow life to pass you by. Deliverance from ungodly soul ties and heartbreak begins with the conviction and realization of its detrimental effects and influences in your life, then a rock solid decision to disassociate from that relationship. Once the choice has been decided, follow through with the Holy Spirit's help. Holy Spirit is with you all the way; in times of vulnerability,

He will wrap you in His strength and enable you can get beyond your emotions and remain secure (Psalm 61:2). Wrong relationships will hinder fulfillment of God's purpose for your life. Yes, it does hurt; but the temporary pain of cutting that person out of your life is worth it to fulfill your real destiny. You are worth it, and you are worth waiting on a God-approved man and relationship. God will never hurt or devalue you; He will not tell you that you can only be with Him at a certain time and place; He is always truthful, always faithful and will always answer your calls. God loves seeing and spending precious time with you; the Lord's scepter is always extended to you at any time!

Esther and all of the virgins were dabbed and massaged with the finest essential oils so that the oils would saturate their pores, soften their skin, so that they become a sweet-smelling aroma to the king. However, the optimum and most essential oil is the oil of the Holy Spirit. There is no oil sweeter, no aroma more alluring than the saturation of Holy Spirit. When you are oiled by Holy Spirit, the fragrance that He smells is Christ. The more you soak in His Presence, the more you become infused with His aroma and the fruit of His ways.

One step in the method of making perfume is to take the flower petals and place them in boiling water for the scent of the flowers to perfume the water. As such, God will take your boiling adversities and perfume your life with His power and make it evident that you are a fragrant beauty of the Lord. Often, the person who hurt you will attempt to come back into your life; but because you have been permeated with the Holy Spirit, the enticing scent of temptation will be a putrid aroma to your nostrils. The infiltrating Presence and fragrance of God will release a victorious aroma that will spread and strengthen you in every situation. *"Not by might nor by power, but by My Spirit, says the Lord of hosts"* (Zechariah 4:6). You will break free from every enslaving relationship, not by your own will power, but by the supply and empowerment of Holy Spirit – your Source and Essential Oil of victory!

Chapter 5

SILVER, GOLD, PEARLS & WISDOM

"Happy the person who finds wisdom, the person who acquires understanding; for her profit exceeds that of silver, gaining her is better than gold, she is more precious than pearls – nothing you want can compare with her." – Proverbs 3:13-15 CJSB

WHILE WE WERE ON A SIBLING'S PRAYER AND discussion conference call, one of our brother's asked for each of us to share any happenings in our lives. As each sibling began to share, I became uneasy and franticly started rehearsing in my mind: "What can I share?" "There is nothing going on." "I have nothing to share." The brother leading the call shared that he applied for a new principal position. Our other brother, who was vice chief of police at the time, shared that he interviewed for the position of chief of police. One of our sisters, a teacher/librarian, shared that she applied at college for a new position. Our other sister had recently been promoted to a supervisor with the postal service. When my turn came to share, I was mentally blank and felt somewhat unsuccessful – as though I was not progressing, so I shared a timid testimony. These thoughts goaded me for days until the Lord highlighted this Scripture: *"For wisdom's profit is better than the profit of silver, and her gain is better than fine gold; She is more precious than rubies; and nothing you can wish for compares with her [in value]"* (Proverb 3:14-15 AMP). The Lord is not promoting lack or poverty; often, we tend to look at wealth as measured *only* by monetary value or income and miss out on the preeminence of spiritual wealth. *"To gain the riches of wisdom is far greater than gaining the wealth of the world"* (Proverbs 3:13c TPT). This kind of wisdom can only be obtained through having a rich relationship with Jesus Christ. This type of wisdom is different from the world's wisdom, which is self-centered and often includes any means necessary to grasp wealth and fame. James describes it as unspiritual and demonic (James 3:15). The world's wisdom is superficial and does not lead to God nor does it promote living righteously for Him. Godly wisdom is a tree of life to those who grasp her and will produce a fountain of blessings (Proverbs 3:18).

Proverbs is replete with sacred sense; it provides understanding and insight of God's wisdom that will empower you to reign in life. The Hebrew meaning of Proverbs has a profound and insightful definition. It means to reign with power, to rule or take dominion. Regardless of your status or financial income, you can reign and take dominion over obstacles and setbacks – any lack – with God's wisdom ruling in your life. It is not too late; listen to the voice of wisdom–the voice of the Holy Spirit directing you in the way to go; instructing in the how's; telling you who to work or connect with. Wisdom is divine counsel from the Holy Spirit; it is reigning sense to prosper.

Happy and blessed is the person who finds and applies skillful and godly wisdom. There is reward in following God's wisdom and there is regret when it is disregarded. I was blessed with a large sum of money and decided to purchase a vehicle. The vehicle I decided on depleted most of the money. Even worse, I did not want my husband to go to the car lot with me nor did I want his signature on the documents – a hard truth to admit. So, I voiced to him unscriptural (carnal) wisdom to make sure things went my way. He came; and as we sat there negotiating with the sales manager, I was trying to think of reasons for him to leave so my intent could be implemented. My husband was aware of my motives; his facial expression is still etched in my mind – disheartened, astounded, injured and speechless. Feeling guilty of my actions, I choose a color for the vehicle that I thought he would like. At that time, we had two vehicles; about one months later after buying the new one, our old car completely stopped working and was not worth fixing. We were back in the same predicament with one car, which he used the majority of the time to go to work and school. Home alone, no transportation, reaping the fruit of my severely selfish, hurtful actions towards my husband. Rather than buying one car, I could have bought two brand new cars – one for each of us and put a portion in savings.

God's Word instructs in wise behavior and imparts spiritual understanding and insight (Proverbs 1:2-3 AMP). Honestly, I did not know that I was so selfish! God used that experience to reveal the specifics of my selfishness and unscrupulous motives, which were rooted in my soul and demonstrated in my behavior. *"And then finally you'll admit that you were wrong and say, "If only I had listened to wisdom's voice and not stubbornly demanded my own way, because my heart hated to be told what to do"* (Proverbs 5:12 TPT). This is an example of the world's wisdom. It does not care about who it hurts as long as it gets its way. The Lord corrected me as a loving father corrects his child. I felt horrible and cried deeply; I was shocked at my conduct! The rod of God's correction was painful, but also good so He could produce virtuous character and the fruit of godly wisdom! *"My child don't underestimate the value of the discipline and training of the Lord God, or get depressed when he has to correct you. For the Lord's training of your life is the evidence of his faithful love. And when he draws you to himself, it proves you are his delightful child"* (Hebrews 12:5 TPT). The Father's nurturing love and sanctifying power was at work within my heart. He was educating me in the school of righteousness and honoring my husband.

"The wise will hear and increase their learning, and the person of understanding will acquire wise counsel and the skill [to steer his course wisely and lead others to the truth]" (Proverbs 1:5). Wisdom (*arts of seamanship*) is like a seaman who assists in the knowledge, operation and skill pertaining to handling, sailing, and navigating a ship during a voyage. Wisdom navigates the courses we should take; it directs our destinations; it is a manager of safety that steers us through the rough and rogue waves of life and points us in the direction of peace and prosperity. Godly wisdom is skillful, precise, practical, specific, safe and strategic. God's wisdoms will guide us through the mazes of life with a productive outcome.

"For the Lord gives wisdom; out of His mouth comes knowledge and understanding" (Proverbs 2:6). The mouth of the Lord is His Word; therefore, God's Word and wisdom are indispensably connected – like needing blood to live. Take this to heart: Get godly wisdom; get understanding and live. Recall the words of wisdom; do not forget one word! Do not swerve an inch; stay on the path that leads to life and safety (Proverbs 4:3-9 MSG). Not exercising godly wisdom leads to immaturity, imprudence and disappointment. It is a serious matter to scoff at the wisdom of God; it will not turn out in your favor (Proverbs 1:30-31 TPT).

"In all your ways acknowledge Him, and He shall direct your paths" (Proverbs 3:6). Notice in the word, ac[know]ledge (Heb. *yada'*) is the word *"know."* This refers to life-giving intimacy, as in marriage. In a spiritual context, it suggests an intimacy with God through the Word, worship and prayer that reveals more of God and produces self-awareness and understanding. When we know God, have direct experiences with Him, He promises to direct our paths toward fruitful, life-producing endeavors. By putting God first, He will navigate you through the hiccups of the day and reveal exactly how to handle the matter at hand. We do not know it all and will need to consult and recognize the One who does and He will cut a straight path before you, clearing the way so you will arrive at your appointed destination.

Beauty Mark

Abigail is a woman who was marked with beauty and sacred intelligence (1 Samuel 25). She was inwardly tattooed with the spirit of wisdom that left an indelible imprint for others to learn and live by. Abigail was in a challenging relationship with her husband Nabal, whose name has a negative connotation – fool, evil, harsh, worthless, wicked – and he lived up to its meaning (1 Samuel 25:25).

David and his men were a wall of protection, day and night, around Nabal's shepherds. He sent some men to tell Nabal of their good deeds, and to ask for food in return for their service. Rather than return good for good and provide them with sustenance, he gave them verbal insults, which caused David to become furious with revenge and vowed that he would kill every male associated with Nabal. One of the shepherds told Abigail what David had said and what Nabal had done. He said to Abigail, *"Now therefore, know and consider what you should do, for evil is plotted against our master and against all his household; and he is such a worthless man that no one can speak to him"* (1 Samuel 25:17). Abigail arose and went into action! No time to waste – without telling Nabal – she immediately prepared donkeys with loads of food and drink for David and his men and instructed her men to go before her. As she was riding her donkey, she met David head on coming from the opposite direction; she quickly dismounted from her donkey, fell on her face before David and bowed herself to the ground (1 Samuel 25:23). She asked for forgiveness though she was not at fault; her husband was a foolish man who would not listen to anyone; nonetheless, she placed herself in a position between life and death. She interceded for her husband's life and all the men who were associated with him. Her intercession and wise discernment kept David from foolishly taking revenge into his own hands, shedding innocent blood, and doing something he would regret later when he became king. She openly agreed with

David that her husband's actions were foolish; yet, humbly reminded him that vengeance belonged to the Lord.

Abigail provided both natural and spiritual food to David; she spoke the truth of God's Word, of who God is, and reminded David of his destiny. God used Abigail to disarm David's anger and keep him from avenging himself. Anger clouded David's good judgment, but God used a beautiful woman marked with His wisdom to influence David to do good rather than evil. Abigail's words were seasoned with grace, insight and understanding; her words ministered to the hearer – David. Wise speech will always be good and beneficial to the progress of others, relating to the necessity and occasion (Ephesians 4:29). The words Abigail spoke were rhema; they spoke to a specific circumstance at a specific time, which manifested the will of God. In faith, she spoke prophetically to David about God fulfilling the promises in his life. Everything that needed to be said by Abigail in that encounter with David was inspired by the Spirit of God. Wisdom speaks the truth; she did not compromise the truth when she spoke with David face-to-face, even though she knew he would become king and was known as a warrior. Is there any one you need to speak the truth in love to without compromise? Have you been withholding what God wants you to say or do?

Abigail met an uninvited, unexpected situation with trust in God and wise behavior. David granted her peace and none of Nabal's men were harmed. Godly wisdom is a path to peace and safety (Proverbs 3:17). At times it is difficult to obey God in stressful situations and deal with the conflict of crucifying the flesh in the midst of urgency. It can be so easy to lose your emotional footing and handle the matter in a way that dishonors God. These moments require meekness (control of one's emotions), discretion and dependence on the Lord. God is a very present help in the times of trouble, and He hears the cries of His people and will be their Succor – come to their rescue.

A quality of intercession, as a spiritual lifesaver, is praying for deliverance and doing what is necessary for the circumstance or persons involved to have a positive outcome. Abigail depicted the actions of a prayer intercessor; she stood between life and death in order to save the lives and destiny of others. When He does, be sure to praise and give honor to Him. The wise will recognize and always give glory to God. David said to Abigail, *"Blessed be the Lord, the God of Israel, who sent you to meet me this day"* (1 Samuel 25:32).

Abigail was a wise and wealthy woman and probably had silver, gold and pearls; and if she did not, she could have purchased them because Nabal was an extraordinarily rich man. However, her greatest asset was her relationship with the Lord. In a life and death matter, she spoke words of wisdom that was a result of having an intimate relationship with God; external responses can demonstrate an internal devotion to God. Wealth alone could not have appeased David's anger; it took a divine intervention of the Lord to bring him to his right senses, and the Words and wisdom of the Lord to stop him from avenging himself with his own hands. David listened to wise counsel, whereas, Nabal did not.

"For her profit is better than the profit of silver. And her gain better than fine gold. She is more precious than jewels; and nothing you desire compares with her. Long life is in her right hand; in her left hand are riches and honor" (Proverbs 3:14-16). Abigail was *wow*! She was both naturally rich

and, more importantly, spiritually rich. She did not allow her wealth to impede her humility and present herself in a prideful manner. Abigail bowed before David; I exhort you to bow before the true and living King Jesus Christ. The Lord, Himself, will raise you up and exalt you in due season.

Godly wisdom will dispense blessings and increase that will launch you into your destiny (Proverbs 3:16). Absorb the Word of God continually; saturate your mind with it to comply with it and have good success (Joshua 1:8). God is for you, not against you. He wants you to thrive; and He delights in prospering you (Psalm 35:27).

Suddenly situations will occur. In every occurrence, you will need God's wisdom to guide your course. It is possible that Abigail's marriage to Nabal was unsatisfying and frustrating because of his harsh temperament. Circumstances may be coming at you from every direction. It may feel as though the enemy has you cornered with your back up against the ropes hitting you with forceful blows. Worship your way through until the breakthrough! Whatever the case, embrace Christ and the value and benefits that godly wisdom produces. Wisdom is far more than the successful operation of knowledge; wisdom is a Person, Jesus Christ, the power and wisdom of God (1 Corinthians 1:24). Whatever the problem is, Jesus is positively the answer to your predicament. It is not a cliché; it is concrete; it is solid; it is Truth! Jesus, the omni-sapient (all-wise) God, is the One with all your solutions and will release rhema wisdom in the specific time of need (Romans 8:28, 37). The divine counsel of God will release both reward and blessings. Abigail was beautiful and wealthy; more significantly, she was rich in godly beauty, character, wisdom, and discernment. She was faithful to God and devoted to her husband, which influenced her right behavior to protect him, despite his wrong actions towards David. By stopping the bloodshed of innocent men and her guilty husband, she identified with being a peace maker (1 Samuel 25:32-34). Matthew 5:9 voices, *"How joyful you are when you make peace! For then you will be recognized as a true child of God"* (TPT). After Nabal's death, David proposed to Abigail; she consented and became King David's wife (1 Samuel 25:36-42).

Woman, you are wow! If Jesus is your Lord and Savior, you are an ambassador of the King of kings. And, through your loyalty to Him, He will brand you with the beauty of godly discernment, garland you with godly character and adorn you with His wisdom, which will cause you to reign in life, display His power and impart peace in turbulent situations. You are called out to represent Him; and you will.

Chapter 6

TREASURED TEARS

"And there was a woman in the city who was a sinner;...bought an alabaster box of very expensive perfume (CJSB)*... and standing behind Him at His feet, weeping, she began to wet His feet with her tears, and kept wiping them with the hair of her head, and kissing His feet and anointing them with perfume"* – Luke 7:38 NASB

UNINVITED, SHE WALKED IN SIMON, THE Pharisee's house to hear and be near Jesus. It was custom when a Rabbi was at a meal the uninvited and the poor were allowed to enter and listen to the gemstones of wisdom. While observing the discussions of the hosts and invited guests, the uninvited were to remain quiet along the walls and stay away from the couches where the conversations occurred. Broken, but grateful to be in His Presence, she disobeyed protocol and walked up closer and stood behind Jesus. She looked upon the One who Love is and tears began streaming down her face onto Jesus' feet. With no cloth in her hand, she used what she had – her hair to wipe her tears from His feet (even though letting her hair down in public was culturally considered immodest). She broke through the confinement of cultural correctness to be close to Jesus. This woman gave Jesus all she had in that moment – true worship. Her tears and humility spoke words that she verbally did not utter. Despite her reputation as a prostitute, regardless of the judgmental chatter and the rejection of religious leaders, in the face of those who counted her as a nobody, she publicly knelt and humbled herself in Jesus' presence and in front of all those who attended the banquet. Love and gratitude to God can cause you to shut out all the boo's and walk pass the stone throwers. Her love for the Lord surpassed the stares, protocol and people's disapproving perceptions to receive exactly what she needed from Jesus – authentic love, unbroken attention, sincere compassion and real comfort.

Despite what you have done in your past, despite what you may be doing now, you have to surpass the fear and shame and move near to Jesus. Nothing you have done can withdraw God's love for you. Yes, the talk of the town was true – she was a woman of the streets, a prostitute. *Was* is key. She did not remain in her sinful condition and lifestyle. Her yielded spirit expressed a new conformity of her heart that responded to the drawing Presence of the Lord. She bowed before Jesus, the lifestyle changer, healer and heart transformer. *"He heals the broken hearted and binds up their wounds healing their pain and comforting their sorrow"* (Psalm 147:3 AMP). Whatever the bondage, addiction, struggle or the amount or kind of immoral acts, God's love has the capacity to break loose chains, liberate you of stigmas, give you a new identity and new ways of living.

The Lord resists the proud but rescues the humble (James 4:6). Pride is an attitude of arrogance and superiority that echoes to God that you are in control. Pride restricts your need of God. Pride is described as wicked and can cause people to exclude God from their lives because they do not esteem and evaluate Him as a vital need (Psalm 10:4). Haughtiness is an enemy of deliverance; it is deceptive and blinding to the conscience. Without humility, salvation is impossible; a contrite spirit is prerequisite to a changed heart, then changed behavior. Pride is like a fortress or barrier that keeps God out and keeps you in prison; there is absolutely nothing positive about self-conceit (Proverbs 8:13, 11:2, 29:23). God's grace is available to be liberated from egotism; but, a refusal of His grace to help will be to our disgrace. Pride is a prophecy of an upcoming downfall (Proverbs 16:18 TPT). God detests it (Proverbs 16:5 TPT).

Broken and weeping, her posture represented a person who is truly penitent for her sins and deeply thankful for redemption. Repentance that excludes humility is a vain confession that is void of the transforming power of God. The love, assurance and security she may have been searching for was found in the one Man, Jesus Christ.

Brokenness before the Lord lifts heavy burdens and breaks iron grips; brokenness is a vital step to your breakthrough. You will find Christ in contrition and humility and experience peace, joy and triumph. This breaking, reliance and submission to God, opens the door for Him to work His will in your life and destroy the continuity and power of sin. Holy Spirit will empower you to disobey the flesh and walk in the spirit of temperance.

Frequently, when something is broken it is often considered worthless and thrown in the trash – not worth fixing. When people are heartbroken and their lives are in disarray, sometimes others consider their lives valueless. Often people believe this about themselves – thinking there is no hope and their life will always be the same. Do not believe the lies. Jesus specializes in broken lives and can restore you to health, healing and wholeness. There is a beauty in brokenness that God delights and moves in. Humility attracts God's attention (Psalm 51:17).

Humility is to be transparent – to be honest. Admitting the truth and applying God's Word will set you free. Truth is the start of a new beginning. *"For if you embrace truth, it will release true freedom into your lives"* (John 8:32 TPT). If truth is to be embrace, you must *know* what the truth is. Truth is God's Word (John 17:17); the Bible is the truth-print by which our lives are piloted. A wide-spread deception and cultural mindset is that love only soothes; it does not conflict with my desires, regardless of what they are. So truth is often dismissed. If something is said that conflicts with this view, you may be categorized as judgmental. The explanation of love has become carnally defined and self-opinionated rather than Bible based (2 Timothy 4:3; 1 Corinthians 13:4-8a AMPC). There is a difference between being judgmental and judging. Judgmental people are condescending, cold-hearted, and often are unforgiving and unloving. Their main aim is to point out mistakes, than to help the person with their problem, which exemplifies a hyper-critical and prideful spirit. Judging is discerning between good and evil in order to determine God's will. This person is influenced by God's love, and offers hope and help to the one in need; yet, does not deny truth. Also, this individual is aware of their vulnerability and need of God's grace and mercy, and remembers God's deliverances in their life (1 Corinthians 6:9-11; Colossians 3:5-10). Bible Truth has the ability to act as a surgeon's scalpel (Hebrews 4:12). Truth can have a cutting effect and does, at times, seem unloving, critical and stinging. Yet these truth-cuts are necessary and are done in God's love. At first, it hurts; later you will learn to appreciate it because it was used to not only change your life, also to save it.

In ancient tradition, women had tear bottles and in those bottles were the tears of their emotional life experiences. Unintentional tears began to shower Jesus' feet and with affectionate tenderness, she kissed His feet again and again as an expression of her reverential love and submission. From her intentional worship, she poured costly perfume on Jesus' feet as a revelational response to who He had become in her life, and what He had done in her heart. She realized the depth of her sin and the greater depths of Jesus' mercy, love, grace and forgiveness (Luke 7:45-47).

She entered Simon's house with the stigma of a prostitute, but exited with the peace of God, wholeness, and in right standing with Him (Luke 7:50).

Chapter 7

WARRIOR PRINCESS "YOU'VE GOT TO FIGHT THIS ONE!"

"Blessed be the Lord, my Rock and my keen and firm Strength, Who teaches my hands to war and my fingers to fight." – Psalm 144:1 AMPC

I AM SURE YOU HAVE HEARD OF THE OLE ADAGE "curiosity killed the cat." I was reminded of this investigative danger when I peered into my teen relative's computer trash can. I said to myself, "Let me see what's in here." I opened his trash and gazed at about 100 deleted hard-core rap songs. There was one rap artist that I had heard a lot about and knew a lot of teens listened to him; personally, I had never heard any of his music. Out of curiosity, I opened one by a popular rap artist, who is now deceased, and the curse words spewed like a sewage breakage. I quickly closed it and emptied everything that was in the trash – thinking that was the end of it. Without realizing, I opened and tapped into a demonic portal.

Later in the night I went into my room to rest, but something felt different; there was a stillness in the atmosphere. Peace was not present, only an errie silence, and regardless of my efforts to sleep, I could not. Soon afterwards, I began hearing voices in the spiritual realm; voices that spoke only vile, putrid hard-core curse words. Never had I experienced anything like that! For two weeks, I prayed almost nonstop without sleep, and because of the lack of sleep, it began to modify my facial appearance. I looked as though I had aged five years and as though I was cousin to a raccoon because of the deep, dark circles around both eyes. The stillness persisted; the satanic voices became louder – even while praying. These voices followed me everywhere – even to the doors of the church they made their presence known. Only when I went inside church did I experience relief and silencing of their voices.

God commanded Barak to gather at Mt. Tabor and take 10,000 warriors from the tribes of Naphtali and Zebulun (Judges 4:6). God gave Barak a strategic plan to fight the battle at Mt. Kishon, the place where the trap was set and their oppressors be baited for defeat; the victory was fixed; but he would not go and fight unless Deborah went with him (Judges 4:7-8). Even though it was not God's original plan, Deborah, fearlessly, agreed to go and participate in the sting operation. So, I preceded to call three people whom I knew had real relationships with the Lord and were spiritual warriors and prophetic people. Two of the people I called for prayer, there was no movement in the spirit; but, the third person, a friend and mentor, when she prayed I sensed movement in the realm of the spirit and some relief. Yet, I did not understand why I was not experiencing the complete breakthrough. Then

I heard the Lord say, *"You've got to fight this one."* Fear tried to keep me from fighting; but I made up my mind to fight and trust God, even though I did not understand all that was happening. In my prayers, I said: "How can I fight the unknown? LORD, I need revelation! I need your strategy! No devil has any business defeating me! LORD, I am your child!"

Shortly afterwards, I laid my head on a pillow to finally get some sleep. The Lord revealed this to me in a dream: I saw two extremely large rats that stood on their hind legs with large dark black marble eyes. One of the rats was in a cage and could not escape. But there was one who was larger and stronger that followed me everywhere in the dream. I turned and faced that rat and asked, "Why are you following me?" There was no reply; but I heard the Lord say, "This kind come out only by prayer and fasting." Prayer alone bound the first unclean spirit. To subjugate the stronger one, I immediately began to unite my prayers with fasting. In the dream I turned and faced that profane spirit, which revealed to me I had to confront and conquer it with faith in Christ and by following His instructions. The Lord reminded me of His Word, *"Listen carefully: I have given you authority [that you now possess] to tread on serpents and scorpions, and [the ability to exercise authority] over all the power of the enemy (Satan); and nothing will [in any way] harm you"* (Luke 10:19 AMP). God has given us His authority to overthrow demonic powers and spiritual enemies. He will use our experiences as a training ground or boot camp for spiritual warfare. Jesus is our General and divine Strategist; He is our Rock, our stability and protection (Psalm 18). There is no weakness in God, and He will provide the strength needed in warfare. Our carnal efforts will not win the battle; God's armor, not ours, will supernaturally equip us with the explosive power needed to oppose demonic assaults (Ephesians 6:10-18). We do not fight like Deborah and Barak did in physical battle; we put our hands and fingers together in prayer and fight the spiritual war. We must be both armed and trained (Genesis 14:14; 2 Samuel 23:8-23). Sometimes, we feel that we are at a disadvantage in warfare because of seemingly insurmountable odds; however, there is no disadvantage in God; we are advantageous in Christ and He, alone, is the Majority. If God stands for you, then who can stand successfully against you? (Romans 8:31). Like David, who slayed Goliath with a sling and a stone (1 Samuel 17:40-50), you will skillfully sling the Word of God and strike the targets. Like Moses, witchcraft and magic will be no match for you (Exodus 7:8-12; 8:16-19). Like Hananiah, Mishael and Azariah fiery circumstances may have you surrounded, but you will not be consumed (Daniel 3:23-25). You can walk in the midst of scorching situations and not be burned; when the enemy launches his attacks, the Lord, strong and almighty, will teach you to fight and put your spiritual enemies to flight.

Sometimes people look at you or overlook you, mistakenly thinking that you are a push over. But what they do not realize is that you are a princess warrior trained by Jehovah Gibbor, the mighty and victorious Man of War! You are a spiritual bomb, a carrier of the dynamite power of God and know how to skillfully execute the Canon – the Word of God. You may not have a public platform, but your personal platform with the Lord makes a divine impact, which has intercepted demonic wiles and schemes that have changed the outcome of people's lives, including yours, and stopped the devil's plans from materializing.

A major component in warfare is God's Word. A woman of war is a woman of the Word! Victory is attached to the Word of God – the belt of Truth. The loin-belt that the Roman soldiers wore in battle was the most significant piece of armor because on this belt hung his shield, sword and lance – weapons of protection and destruction to counteract and defeat their enemies. These tools were kept close at hand in combat so that whatever weapon was needed to gain the advantage, it was right there at his disposal. As it is with spiritual warfare, God will release rhema to your spirit – a specific revelatory Word of God for your specific situations that must be declared to overthrow the opposition. Rhema acts as an archer that hits the target; it is a sharpshooter of accuracy. Going into battle without the loin belt described an unprepared soldier whose defeat was certain. Separation or absence of God's Word in spiritual combat is a casualty. It takes fight and faith to fulfill God's purpose and your future is worth the fight, and so is your family's bloodline.

Faith, bold confidence in God, is a safeguard against our adversaries and a shield to quench Satan's fiery darts against us (Ephesians 6:16).

Studying the Scriptures have taught me to enforce Jesus' already-won victory; to persist in prayer and the importance of prophetically declaring and decreeing God's Word. Also, living righteously will block breaches of unholy living and prevent Satan from gaining an advantage or foot-hole by cracking your breastplate of righteousness (Ephesians 6:14 TPT; 4:27 AMPC). The warfare with those two unclean spirits was a boot camp of personal training and skill. The outcome was what God originally expected – total victory!

Some battles we call others to war with us; when we need to ask for help, call on the people of war (Joshua 8:1). A leader of a ministry asked me to intercede for the needs of their church. At first, I was surprised because I was not a member; but I said to God that if this prayer assignment is Your will, I will do it. About two days later, I began interceding for the needs, increase and success of the church. One Sunday, while visiting their church, at the end of the service I felt a strong wave of a spirit flow over me. It felt so strange; I began feeling woozy. It was even difficult walking to my car; because, it felt as though I was going to fall. I walked sideways as if I were drunk; I could not walk in a straight line. The next day, while still feeling that awful presence, I decided to go to the bookstore. When I got there, I had to sit on the floor of the bookstore to continue looking at the books because I could not stand without wavering. I realized that because I was interceding for the church, the warfare turned against me. It was a territorial spirit with the characteristics of an alcoholic; alcohol addiction is problem in this area.

Because of the strength of the battle, I recognized that I needed backup; I needed another warrior to fight with me. I called a seasoned prophetess and told her the details. Her exact words were, "Good God Almighty! That is a strong spirit and the reason I felt it everywhere I went because it was following me! And, that God is going to answer your prayers about the church." We came together in agreement, spiritual warfare and prophetic prayer! The power of deliverance was manifested. Even afterwards, I was still experiencing some dizziness, though not as much.

Regardless of this, I knew God used her to intercept the devil's plans, and that I had to continue standing in faith and declaring the Word of God. *"Though one may be overpowered by another, two can withstand him. And a threefold cord is not quickly broken"* (Ecclesiastes 4:12 NKJV). Christ is the unbreakable cord that binds us in unity, power and strength. Within two or three days all of the symptoms and signs of that evil presence vanished, and the victory manifested both for the me and the ministry.

When you are in spiritual warfare, you need people with a spirit like Naphtali; these people know how to wrestle and throwdown and dethrone the enemy. And, those with a spirit like Zebulun, who will believe God with you and exalt His Word concerning the matter. Other battles we are called by God to war alone as He teaches and trains our hands to war and our fingers to fight, He is the One who gives strength and skill for the battle (Psalm 144:1 TPT).

Princess warrior, either way, alone or with others, as it was with Deborah, whose name means bee, your victory is sweet as honey!

Chapter 8

DECEPTIVE BEAUTY

The rulers of the Philistines went to her and said, "Entice Samson to tell you what makes him so strong and how he can be overpowered and tied up securely. Then each of us will give you 1,100 pieces of silver." – Judges 16:5 NLT

S
HE WAS YOUNG IN THE FAITH, IMMATURE IN godly wisdom and lacked knowledge of spiritual things; but she loved God with all of her heart. In her pursuit to grow in the things of God, she went to a new ministry where she thought she could draw closer to God and grow spiritually. She witnessed the gifts of the Spirit on a different scale and realm that she had never seen or experienced. The leader of the ministry was both lion-hearted and lamb-like. She settled in her mind that this is where she was supposed to be and was never leaving; she was active in the ministry and loved being there and thought nothing could change that.

Married, living like a single woman, and rejected by her husband (former), this place (church) filled those absent places in her heart. She felt such fulfillment and began thinking about the Pastor day and night and how mightily God used him. While lying in bed thinking about the Pastor, her husband came to the house – he never lived there – walked in the room where she was and said, "Who are you in love with?" Eyes widened, she said "no one!" Then he said, "Who are you infatuated with?" Her soul trembled as she repeated "infatuated," and realized that it described me! Lying and petrified to admit the truth, "I said no one!" Alarmed, I asked, "God am I infatuated with him?" Everything pointed to "yes." I was mesmerized by the gifts of operation in this person's ministry; I focused so much on how God used him in preaching, prophesying and the word of knowledge without realizing it was an open door for satanic influence and control.

One night I decided to attend a revival at another ministry. After the service, I walked outside with a woman, who is a prophetess and as we were talking, she said to me, *"You can't handle sin."* I intuitively knew what she was referring to. Those words became my meditation. I thought about the consequences of making the wrong decision. It would break up and destroy families: his family, the church family, my family and it would be publicized. The after-shock would have been utter destruction and devastating; the pain would have been off the scale! The thought of being the cause, the woman, of this turmoil was too much for me to bear. And, the thoughts of great displeasure to God overwhelmed me.

So much I did not understand. I pondered as to why was I experiencing these feelings and having these thoughts? I did not want to have those feeling! I knew it was wrong! He was married with children and I was married with children too. Yet a compelling, a persuading force, was there at every waking and sleeping moment! The temptation was fiercely intense, and I needed help! I was so naïve; I did not have the sense to leave the ministry. So, I thought that I needed to confess this to the Pastor; and I did. I assumed he would call upon some of the wiser women of the church to gather around me and pray; that did not happen. He asked, "Do you feel this way about anyone else?" My reply was "no." I said to him that I should leave the church; he disagreed. Attracted, confused and challenged, I remained.

Tempted and terrified, I prayed and cried out to God with all my heart for His help; it was a 911 situation. "God, help me! I don't want to fall! Don't let me succumb to the pressure!" The Lord heard me and answered my desperate cries! God's rhema Word was my succor and strength. Holy Spirit led me to read Psalm 121:

> *I will lift up my eyes to the hills; from whence comes my help?*

> *My help comes from the LORD, Who made heaven and earth.*

> *He will not allow your foot to be moved; He who keeps you will not slumber.*

> *Behold, He who keeps Israel shall neither slumber nor sleep.*

> *The Lord is your keeper; The Lord is your shade on your right hand.*

The sun will not smite you by day, nor the moon by night.

The Lord will protect you from all evil; He will keep your soul.

The Lord will guard your going out and your coming in from this time forth and forever.

Whenever I needed to meet with him in his office, this same lady always showed up and came in the office within minutes. Somewhat irritated, I thought, the Pastor and I are talking! Why is she in here? Still, I did not give much attention as to why she always showed up. I realized later, by her admission, that she had been praying for me and keeping watch over me. Wow! God had an intercessor praying for both of us, as well as watching and intervening when she saw potential danger. Peace flooded my soul; I had the needed confidence that God is my anchor and protector. And, even in times of soul-shaking temptations, He is able to safeguard me from all evil.

Watchmen and intercessors sleep; but, the divine Watchman and Guardian does not and absolutely nothing can sneak in unaware or catch Him by surprise. Twenty-four hours per day, seven days per week, we are under the Lord's watch care and protection. A covenant-keeper portrays the Lord; therefore, He will not alter the utterances of His lips (Psalm 89:34). He kept me from stumbling and saved me from a great fall; He is able to keep you from falling too (Jude 1:24).

Delilah used lust, persistence and manipulation to coax Samson, the strong man, into revealing the secret of his strength. Delilah never loved Samson; her pretended affection was a performance or play-act only to receive the money she was promised from chief Philistines (Judges 16:5). She wore Samson down with her constant nagging and pressured him until he revealed everything about the secret of his strength – a Nazarite from birth and no razor was to touch his head (Judges 16:15-18). He lost sight of his purpose and revealed the secret of his strength to a woman whose name means feeble. Delilah had a secret too; she secretly made a pact with the Philistines to enfeeble and enslave Samson. His strength was in his consecrated covenant relationship with God, of which his hair was a symbol. Their method of bribery played out through their seductress of deception – Delilah. She had Samson just where she wanted – duped, snared and weak (Judges 16:19). She used the word "love" to charm him, *"How can you say, 'I love you,' when your heart is not with me?"* (Judges 16:15). This word has been used in the past and present for self-centered purposes and afterwards the victim feels abused, ashamed and angry. The lips of a seductress are compared to the sweetness of a honeycomb, and her words smoother than oil (Proverbs 5:1-23; 31:30). Delilah's flattering words and double-dealing actions pierced and cut him like a double-edge sword. Romancing an enemy exposed Samson's vulnerability and achieved his captivity. Ladies, some relationships are off-limits; in other words, do not go there – to the place of temptation. Samson's cut hair signified a detachment of his dedication to God; consequently, the Lord departed too (Judges 16:19). Engaging in illicit relationships will cut-off your relationship with the Lord; continuing in this practice can affect your sensitivity to the Holy Spirit's convictions. Forbidden relationships, as described in the Bible, has not changed and never will.

Satan desired to use me as a modern-day Delilah – to bring down the strong man. The minister was making a great impact that was transforming people's lives and the enemy wanted to put a stop to it; so, he devised a plan that would have damaged and shattered many lives. This man was a real, Spirit-empowered servant of God and Satan wanted to use me as a tool of enticement to cause his demise and cease kingdom advancement. At this ministry, many people were accepting Jesus Christ as their Lord and Savior; and truth was powerfully preached without compromise.

Transparency is characteristic of a WOW woman. Some things are mortifying and difficult to admit; but it is necessary for God's help and deliverance. We have an accountability to God, others and ourselves.

On no occasion, use your beauty, body and influence to mislead and betray anyone – use methods of seduction to bait and trap. This demeans your character and misrepresents your worth and value. This is hazardous and it is not advantageous. *"She has prevented many from considering the paths of life. Yes, she will take you with her where you don't want to go, sliding down a slippery road not even realizing where the two of you will end up!"* (Proverbs 5:4-5 TPT). You will not gain from a wife's tears, nor being a factor in causing a family to fail. It may feel like a win. In actuality, it is a lost and it is not the ways of God. This does not release the man involved of his accountability and responsibility; however, decide to take the high-way and not the valley of hardship. God will not tell you that a married man is your husband.

Choices reap consequences either negative or positive. We need God's grace to make the right decisions when tempted to do wrong and the courage to say "yes" or "no" at the right times, regardless of who the person is. It is essential that we have inner grit or integrity, which is having the moral bravery and substance to stand by your godly convictions and having the grit to make right decisions followed by righteous application. Integrity is lived while in public audiences as well as in private settings. Integrity includes being whole, undivided, complete, unaffected and void of hypocrisy. Grit is to have firmness of character or an indomitable spirit. We all stand at the crossroad of decisions, which Satan desires to use these moments to get us to deviate and take bypaths (alternate ways); but *"This is what the LORD says: Stand at the crossroads and look; ask for the ancient paths, ask where the good way is, and walk in it, and you will find rest for your souls"* (Jeremiah 6:16). The Lord exhorts us to travel on the highway of holiness, which is founded on the unchangeable character of His Word – not on the opinions of popular people or polls.

Severe any ties associated with being Delilah's daughter (having her attributes); this is not God's purpose for you. Taking on characteristics of Delilah subjects you to being used as an object rather than a precious, valuable daughter of Sarah. You may think you are in the driver's seat; but you are not. Satan is in the driver's seat using you as his servant to manipulate men, even godly men – married or single (Romans 6:12-18; 8:12 TPT). Sin has a voice; refuse to answer its call. You were created for noble purposes – honorable works. God will never approve of anything contrary to His Word or character. When you manipulate someone, it is usually premediated and planned for self-centered gain; it is done with an intent to mislead, which originates from impure motives. A manipulative woman uses cunning compliments to conceal her motive and to seize what she wants, as Delilah did.

Satan is a master of deception and manipulation, and of injecting seemingly profitable thoughts rooted in lies. He is a master of disguise and masquerades as an angel of light (2 Corinthians 11:14). He fools you to think that you are in control; concretely, he is in control piloting your life. When Delilah saw that Samson's strength was gone, she began to torment him (Judges 16:19); her motives were achieved. *"A bad motive can't achieve a good end; double-talk brings you double trouble"* (Proverbs 17:20 MSG). She left Samson for dead, derided and defenseless. Satan is constant in his pursuit of leashing havoc, confused identity and false purpose.

Daughter of Sarah, beloved of God, your true purpose and identity is realized only in God – your Creator. Sarah's daughters are women of faith who allow the Holy Spirit to produce the fruit of repentance in their lives. *"So, produce fruit that is consistent with repentance [demonstrating new behavior that proves a change of heart, and a conscious decision to turn away from sin]"* (Matthew 3:8). Jesus and John proclaimed repentance. Repent is not a bad word; at the root of repentance is God's love. It is the route to reconciliation with Father God. Repentance is an act of God's grace that will lead to a new life of freedom in Christ and forgiveness. Repentance is a point of access to the Lord; it invites God into your heart and lifts heavy burdens. It is a place of mercy, cleansing, restoring and order (Psalm 51). God's forgiveness and Christ's finished work distances you from sin, and its power, and draws you near to Him. Real repentance reaches the throne and heart of God. Therefore, Holy Spirit conviction is necessary because it is the channel of conversion and change. God does not give truth to merely provide information; He wants transformation – the fruit of repentance to be evident in our lives – holy character to fulfill his holy callings.

There are ungodly images and persuasions all around us and the pressure to conform according to the script of this world. Daughters of Sarah, our script does not come from this world, but from the Holy Scriptures. Be bold to live holy. First Peter 3:6b (TPT) explains that we are Sarah's daughters if we do what is right and yield to no panic. In other words, when you reverently fear God, you do not have to fear any other kind of fear. You are not a daughter of Delilah – mistaken identity. Be audacious to live like a daughter of Sarah; and refuse to use your freedom to violate your freedom in Christ. You are God's special treasure of great importance set apart as His devoted one (1 Peter 2:9).

The most significant beauty of Sarah's daughters come from within. Styles and fashions come and go; appearances and hairstyles can change. But there is a beauty that has a lasting effect; it is an internal and eternal beauty of the heart – an unfading loveliness. Pretty clothes can turn people's head; but a heart submitted to Jesus Christ can influence lives with God's love that can turn their eternal destiny in the right direction. You can be bold, beautiful and holy (1 Peter 3:4).

During that time of temptation, it was no accident that the Holy Spirit placed thoughts of Samson and Delilah in my mind. It was like looking into a mirror and what I realized caused me to shudder in my soul! The Lord provided an exodus, a way of escape, to prevent me from being overcome by temptation. He severed the detrimental association and completely uprooted me from that ministry – something I assumed would never happen – to keep me and those involved safe. *"No test or temptation that comes your way is beyond the course of what others have had to face. All you need to remember is that God will never let you down; he'll never let you be pushed past your limit; he'll always be there to help you come through it"* (1 Corinthians 10:13 MSB). God's grace was sufficient through it all and He proved it with victorious results.

Chapter 9

LOVE WARRIOR

"Then Jesus made a public spectacle of all the powers and principalities of darkness, stripping away from them every weapon and all their spiritual authority and power to accuse us. And by the power of the Cross, Jesus led them around as prisoners in a procession of triumph. He was not their prisoner; they were His!" – Colossians 2:15 TPT

GOD WENT TO EXTREME, DEMONSTRATIVE acts to prove His love for us; the proof is through the life and death of His Son, Jesus. He gave His life for us – no one took it – for people with worth, value, purpose and potential. What is so amazing about God's love is that He sent Jesus to die for us while we were doing our own thing – waddling in sin and excluding Him from our lives. Simply put, God's love for us did not depend on our own accomplishments, merits or positive responses towards His love. Jesus' love is so radical that He did not permit the indescribable pain of being beaten with a whip that was made with broken glass and bones to break Him, nor the thorn of crowns to crush Him, nor spitting and plucking out His beard to subdue Him, nor the mocking to mortify Him, nor deathly agony cause Him to abandon His assignment, nor a kiss of betrayal influence Him to backup, nor the Crucifixion to sway Him. I think, the greatest distress Jesus felt was when He uttered with a loud cry, *"Eli! Eli! L'mah sh'vaktani? That is, My God! My God! Why have you deserted Me?"* (Matthew 27:46 CJSB). This anguishing cry was a deep expression of abandonment and rejection Jesus felt by the Father as He bore the sins of the world. Not only had Jesus never sinned; He never experienced separation from the Father until it became a matter of our salvation and reconciliation for humanity. Jesus' love for us was unstoppable! He was relentless in His focus and would not be detoured nor allow any pauses to conflict with His purpose. His fervent passion and sacrificial love for people far surpassed all that He endured.

Many mistakenly think that Jesus was a push-over – a weakling; He was not weak, Jesus exemplified temperance, an exercising of self-restraint. For instance, John 18:1-4 reveals that Jesus went to the Garden of Gethsemane to pray knowing very well that He would be taken captive there. He knew that Judas, the Roman soldiers and temple police, along with officers of the high priest and Pharisees would come there to arrest Him. Think about this: The soldiers that accompanied Judas, the betrayer, was comprised of 500-600 armed men with swords and spears went to arrest one Person. When they arrived, Jesus went to the garden's entrance, stepped forward and asked, *"Whom do you want?"* Jesus of Nazareth was their reply. Jesus proclaimed, *"I AM He."* At the declaration of *I AM,* the strong men went backward from Him and fell with a powerful force to the ground. All of the soldiers and temple police were knocked flat on the ground by this one Man Jesus. The authoritative and omnipotent Word of God was being demonstrated! Jesus revealed His divinity and proved to them He could not be taken by force. Additionally, Jesus asked, *"Or do you suppose that I cannot call on My Father, and at once He will place at My side twelve legions of angels?* (Matthew 26:5-54 Tree of Life Bible). This would have been 72,000 angels of war – an army of men versus angelic warriors. In the Old Testament, one angel of the Lord struck down 185,000 Assyria soldiers (Isaiah 37:36). Jesus, Adonai-Tzva'ot, the God of the armies of Israel, was all-sufficient without angelic assistance. Yet, He chose not to cause His own release, and Jesus accepted suffering because it was all a part of the Father's plan. Willingly, Jesus permitted the soldiers to take Him captive with the full knowledge of what awaited Him. His captivity was crucial so we could be freed from the imprisonments of sin and bondages. This captivity, eventually led to the crucifixion, which was required from Father God to offer us His most precious gift of salvation. God so loved us that He had to demonstrate it by giving His Son; His love for us could not be contained; it had to be displayed! Through Yeshua (Jesus), God's love was fully revealed through the shedding of His blood, suffering, death and resurrection (John 3:16; Ephesians 2:13*). "For God made Christ, who never sinned, to be the offering for our sin, so that we could be made right with God through Christ"* (2 Corinthians 5:21). Put another way, Jesus took our wrongs so we could become right with God. Without any stipulations from us, Jesus willingly gave His very life so those who choose Him could have eternal life and live the life He planned for them in the earth! Another way to say this is, "Your best life begins with Jesus Christ."

Jesus' death was not an act of defeat; it was an act of total 100% victory! His self-less life proved that nothing and no one has the power to destroy or defeat Him. Love and obedience to the Father were foremost driving factors. The Love Warrior, Yeshua (Jesus), radically demonstrated His love for us in His glorious resurrection – bursting and breaking through death, and defeating spiritual darkness – evil powers, principalities, rulers and most of all the lead prince of destruction and deception – Satan.

First Corinthians 13:7 describes love this way: *"If you love someone, you will be loyal to him no matter what the cost. You will always believe in him, always expect the best of him, and always stand your ground in defending him"* (TLB).

Don't Leave Love Behind

Being that love is a leading motive of Jesus for all that He did, so it must be a main motive for all that we do too. *"Let everything you do be done in love [motivated and inspired by God's love for us]"* (1 Corinthians 16:14 AMP). *The Amplified Classic edition, explains it this way:* ..."*(true love for God and man as inspired by God's love for us)."*

Opposition and offense can cause us to stutter-step towards walking in love or hinder us from loving as we should. Disagreements and wrong doings happen to us all; at times we have been the main cause. Conflicts are a major cause of division and dependent on the insult, we may allow our love for the offender to be withheld or it becomes a determining factor whether we will forgive and demonstrate love towards that person(s). I have seen so many families who have turned their backs on each other and have vowed they will never speak with their own sister, brother, mother, father or long-time friend; the list goes on. I am not upholding any wrongdoings; however, I am upholding the Word and the love of God.

Paul said, ..."*forgetting those things which are behind, and reaching forth unto those things which are before*... (Philippians 3:13). When something is forgotten, it is no longer an issue and does not manifests itself anymore in the form of offense, setbacks, relational irritability or unproductivity. Yet, it is relevant because you learn from it. You have paused the upsetting memories, stopped thinking about it, and put a halt to the hurts that accompany it.

Love is different. Love is never obsolete, outdate, antiquated or irrelevant; love always applies whatever the circumstance. Love is never to be left behind. It is always relevant, always inclusive – like a magnet gravitates to metal. Love is always connected to God's people. Love is the magnetic force that draws people to Him. *"Love never fails [never fades out or becomes obsolete or comes to an end]"* (1 Corinthians 13:8 AMP). Love is always in the equation.

Nearing the end and entering a new year, we tend to evaluate our achievements, things that did not materialize as we hoped, reflect on new goals and desires such as marriage, business, ministry, etc. In this new list of desires or old ones, has *agape* love been included? Are you reaching forth to love as God desires you to? Reaching forth is running towards a goal, an achievement. It denotes a runner in a race running with every ounce of strength he can muster to get to the winner's tape first. It is a vision in view. It is aiming our focus on receiving our heart's desires, as we diligently work towards achieving it. With a runner the race comes to an end. With Love, it never does. God is eternal; therefore, love is eternal.

"Eagerly pursue and seek to acquire [this] love [make it your aim, your great quest]" (1 Corinthians 14:1a AMPC). Love is a fuel that acts as a guide for our lives. If you are not motivated by love, then you are not motivated by God. Love is a Wow factor and a crown characteristic of Christ and Christianity (John 13:35).

"Go after a life of love as if your life depended on it—because it does" (MSG). To pursue love is like *"hunters in a chase."* Strive for love with every means in your power. Love opens the true way to everything else. Without God's love operating in us, people cannot see God and we have not surrendered to God as we should.

God has graced and blessed us with varieties of gifts and talents; an awesome distinction is that we do not all have the same gifts and callings. Yet, God has called us all to love Him and one another (John 13:34; Ephesians 5:2). Love is not title-dependent nor is it opinion-oriented nor based on how people respond to us – positively or negatively.

You may think, "But, you don't know what he or she did to me." No, I do not; but God does. For safety purposes, it is wise to distance ourselves from injurious relationships. Even still, those who have hurt us, we cannot harbor hate and refuse to love them. For instance, God despises sin; but He loves the sinner and gives repentant ones opportunities to ask for forgiveness. God's unconditional love has never been dependent on our favorable responses towards Him.

Some people are categorized as hard cases to love. Love can also mature and bear more fruit by relational tough cases. A condensed version: One of my daughter's teen years, (both were noncompliant in their own way), was described as rebellious, disrespectful, prideful, pregnant and deceptive. I did not comprehend why she was so defiant; I was baffled. She took me through so much emotional turmoil – to the point of turning my back on her. I was on the brink – one decision away – of totally disassociating myself with my very own daughter. We did not experience a loving mother-daughter relationship; it was mostly filled with resistance. For many years, I carried a painful and deep longing in my heart for us to be close. On the contrary, dislike, displeasure and unforgiveness was on the other side of that desire. I did not discuss my pre-meditated decision with the Lord; I pondered it in my heart. Then, one day, a turning point happened. The omniscient Lord said to me, *"I did not turn my back on you. So, how are you going to turn your back on her?"* This changed my course; I am so thankful to God! Love does not stop loving; it is constant. God's love will challenge the *quit* in you. Love is not blinking – it does not turn on and off like a light switch. I almost gave up on my daughter. Had I not chosen to love my daughter in spite of the constant conflicts, I would not have been living as a true disciple of the Lord. Hate breeds death, love breed life. Love does not stare at evil (evil eye), meaning all you can see in someone is the negative. Holding offense fences in the injury, which cause even more injury, and places a fence between you and the offender. Love will see the offense, but choose to overlook it, learn from it, and focus on what is good and refuse to hold resentment. Love does not desire ill wishes on others. Love is a peacemaker in relationships that will break barriers of hate, indifference and remorselessness (1 Corinthians 13:4-8 AMP/NLT).

Press on toward the goal to love; aim at it; run after it; let love be your highest goal. Running after love is pursuing God! God is Love; so, the definition of it, the qualities of it, the grace to walk in it comes from Him. Love is a quality that Christians are known by. John 13:35 utters, *"For when you demonstrate the same love I have for you by loving one another, everyone will know that you're My followers"* (TPT).

Jesus, the Love Warrior is the demonstrative, expressed image of Father God's *agape* love. Jesus' life was an exhibition of love and affection for humanity, which serves as irrefutable proof that He loves you and endured willful suffering at the cost of His own life to prove it! (1 Corinthians 13:7). Agape portrays the highest form of love; it describes the Love Warrior, who could not contain it. Love moved the Lover to action. Nothing would stop Him, and nobody could block Him from displaying God's reliable, relentless, radical love for you.

Chapter 10

GOD, WHO SEES ME

"Then she called the name of the LORD who spoke to her, "You are God Who Sees"; for she said, "Have I not even here [in the wilderness] remained alive after seeing Him [who sees me with understanding and compassion]?"
– Genesis 16:13 AMP

I T HAD BEEN TEN YEARS SINCE THEY HAD SET-tled in the land of Canaan. In Sarai's logic it was too late to conceive at her age to birth the child of promise; Abram was even older. So, Sarai took matters into her own hands; and in her plan of action, she convinced Abram to take Hagar as his substitute wife and bear children through her. After all, the children would be considered hers. In her desperation, Sarai succumbed to the customs of that era, which was considered acceptable. Although it was an acceptable practice, her plan was not written in the blueprint of God. Be careful not to make major decisions from a soul filled with frantic. For example, fearful and with seemingly no other alternative (catch 22), I literally signed my house away for nothing in return and without knowing where I would go from there. My house was in the process of foreclosure and my former spouse refused to help. The buyer of the house said to me, "It's like taking candy from a baby." I felt bamboozled, like a foolish child.

My decision was imprudent; still God sent help. One day as my dad was driving by my house, he saw the for-sale sign; snatched it up and paid for me to get the deed back to my house. God, thank you! Even though it was several years ago, I recollect the lesson.

"So, Sarai said to Abram, 'Look now, the LORD has prevented me from bearing children. Please go to my maidservant; perhaps I can build a family by her.' Abram listened to the voice of Sarai." (Genesis 16:2 Berean SB). It partially happened as Sarai devised; her maid did become pregnant; but she did not expect Hagar to look at her with contempt and despise her. Otherwise speaking, Hagar viewed Sarai as insignificant and an object of disgrace. Fleshly ideas will never produce God's results; His promises accompany His own methods (Proverbs 3:5-7 AMP). Consequently, Abram gave Sarai permission to deal with Hagar as she pleased. Angry, hurt and frustrated, *"Sarai treated her harshly and humiliated her"* (Genesis 16:9).

Hagar could not withstand the treatment any longer and ran away from Sarai into the wilderness (Genesis 16:7). Alone by a spring in the desert, the Angel of the Lord came to aid her. He asked, *"Where have you come from and where are you going?"* Hagar replied, *"I am running away from my mistress Sarai."* She knew where she had come from; but, did not know where she was going; she was at a standstill – no answer (Genesis 16:8).

Why would an omniscient God (Psalm 147:5) ask questions? After all, His understanding is inexhaustible.

For certain, He does not ask questions because He is seeking information; He asks questions to give us information and revelation. Some other reasons are: for us to look deep within ourselves to pinpoint the root causes of our actions (awareness); expose character flaws; circumstances that need to be changed; He reveals His identity and divinity in ways we have not known or understood; and He rebukes in the form of questions. His questions cause introspection, which can lead to divine instructions, reprimand, reconciliation and restoration; and if obeyed, blessings. His purposes for asking differs based on the situation and the needs of the one to whom the question is directed. God's questions will always be based on His plans and will for our lives. His questions are like a bow and arrow that hits to the heart of the matter – precisely.

Have you ever felt unnoticed or unheard by God? Forgotten? And said something like: "God! do you see what I am going through?" "Where are You?" "Do You care?" "I'm hurting." "Why?" "When"? "What?" Our questions to God can be numerous and time can seem like an enemy – especially when your heart's desire is still in waiting, what seems like forever. Uncertainty can boggle your mind with doubting thoughts, such as: "I thought God said..." "Maybe God changed His mind." "Maybe I missed it." "Did God really say...?" "It's too late; I'm in my 30s, 40s, 50s, 60s..." "God, this is taking too long." Age does not place any limitations on God; not trusting Him limits your faith and lessens peace. God will use times of waiting to develop patience (endurance) and to stretch our faith to believe beyond circumstances and what we see, hear or feel. During the wait, we sometimes wrestle with weed attitudes that God brings to surface that need to be uprooted;

and this can take time. Cooperate with the process while change is occurring in the waiting period. Trust that God always knows what He is doing even when we at time do not; trust and time hold hands. The just lives by faith and those who live by faith lives life trusting God and will not be ashamed. People disappoint; circumstances can be disappointing; but there is no disappointment in Him. *"They cried out to You and were delivered; they trusted in You and were not disappointed or ashamed"* (Psalm 22:5 AMPC). The Lord is a loving, covenant-keeping, prayer answering God. He sees you; He has not forgotten about you – no, never. Even though Zion (Jerusalem) caused her own captivity, they cried out to the Lord:

> *"But Zion (Jerusalem in captivity) said, The Lord has abandoned me, and my Lord has forgotten me.*
>
> *[The Lord answered] "Can a woman forget her nursing child and have no compassion on the son of her womb?*
>
> *Even these may forget, but I will not forget you.*
>
> *Indeed, I have inscribed [a picture of] you on the palms of My hands;*
>
> *Your city walls [Zion] are continually before Me."*
>
> (Isaiah 49:14-16 AMP).

You are perpetually before the Lord. No circumstance can hide you from His face; He sees you; His eyes are always upon you; and His tender love for you is unending. No one can change His mind about you. You are permanently imprinted on the palm of His hands; which is a strong testament of God's compassionate watch care and assurance that you are always on His mind. God's love is tattooed all over you; and it cannot be erased.

Time or tribulations cannot thwart God's Word concerning your welfare (Jeremiah 29:11). *"And the LORD remembered Sarah as He had said, and the LORD did unto Sarah as He had spoken"* (Genesis 21:1 JPS Tanakh 1917). Sarah at age 90 and Abraham at 100 years old, birthed the child of prophecy and promise just like God said they would. God would not prevent His promise from being birthed.

Just as the Lord did with Hagar, He will meet you in your wilderness experience, a place where it appears that nothing good is happening – dry, silent, barren, bewildered, and heated with frustrations. Distrust can cause stormy situations to cloud your view and cause you to question if God is doing anything, or make it seem as though there is no solution or sunny days ahead. Where is the rainbow – the manifestation of what God said He would do? Even in the desert, there was a spring – a well called Beer Lahai Roi, which means "well of the Living One who sees me." It was a place of seeing. In the wilderness was where God gave Hagar revelation of her posterity. (Genesis 16:10-12). *"Because the Lord has heard and paid attention to your persecution (suffering)* (Genesis 16:11). The Angel of the Lord told Hagar that she was pregnant and to name her son Ishmael, which means *God pays attention* – a guarantee that God saw her plight.

The Lord was aware of Sarah's (Sarai) barrenness and Hagar's home situation. The Lord graciously remembered them both; and He, *El Roi* (God who sees), graciously remembers you too and will do exactly what He promised you.

Sarah thought it was humorous when she heard the Lord say she would have a baby; saying to herself, " *Shall I really give birth [to a child] when I am old?"* (Genesis 18:13). The Lord *heard* her; and irrespective of her response, He declared that at the appointed time she will give birth to Isaac. Facts are not a factor against God's Words – they do not alter what He said. Abraham laughed (Genesis 17:17); and Sarah laughed (Genesis 18:12). The Angel of the Lord told Abraham to name their son Isaac, which means laughter and proved that nothing is too complicated for Him (Genesis 18:14, 21:2).

Lord, I Want My Baby

Sixteen and single, unwedded and afraid, the pregnancy test was positive. Only my boyfriend and I knew the results. I kept this information hidden for almost three months; but the time came when I could not hide it any longer – my tummy had gotten larger; I had to tell it all. To break the news, I decided that it would be easier to write a letter of confession and put it in a visible place to be sure the letter would be noticed and read.

Before that, I went to a well-known organization thinking I would find consolation and positive reinforcement, only to discover their only option was abortion. My last statement to that counselor was "I'm keeping my baby."

I began being pressured and coerced to have an abortion by an authority figure – something I certainly did not want to do. I wanted to reach out for help; but I did not know where to turn. I felt so helpless and assumed that I had no other choice.

The appointment was scheduled. We arrived at the place to terminate my child; and as we were sitting there, my eyes filled and overflowed with uncontrollable tears of helplessness. So, I walked to the bathroom and cried non-stop. Soon afterwards, the person who brought me to the clinic, came into the bathroom and said to me "stop crying because if the doctor sees you crying, he may not do the procedure." So, I steadied myself and did as I was told. Against my will, I had the abortion.

Days following, I pretended as though nothing happened – laughing at things that were not funny. My happiness was mocked; it was a cover up. The truth of my real state of being came to the forefront; I could not fake it any longer. Even though I functioned and related with people well, inside I was grief-stricken, empty, and felt as though I had been raped. I ached in my heart to hold my baby. It was so painful to see the milk flowing from my breasts, and no baby to suckle. It was extremely difficult for me to let go. I wanted my baby! Thirty years had passed; still every time I thought about my child – even at times when I was driving – I wept sorely. The emotional wounds were deeply heart-wrenching.

I was employed as an administrative assistant and prayer counselor at a well-known church in Fort Lauderdale, FL. While at work one day, I received a phone call from a woman who called the prayer line periodically to ask for prayer; but this time she called to pray for me and convey a message from the Lord. The prayer and Word of the Lord focused on the long-term grief and that God was healing me! Honestly, I do not think I asked God to heal me from the pains of my past; I assumed it was something that was a part of me, and I just had to deal with it as it came.

The Lord used someone, from a different state, who I never shared my painful experiences of having an abortion; nor did I personally know her as a friend. He used this good Samaritan to release the healing power and presence of His Word to manifest the deep healing that I needed. God is the *God Who Sees,* and He came to my rescue and met every need.

Abortion is a sensitive subject, and a much-debated topic. However, God's Word is clear on the matter (Exodus 20:13; Deuteronomy 30:19; Job 31:15; Psalm 22:1, 139:13-16; Proverbs 6:16-19). Seek the Lord on this matter, He will unfold to you what He honors and dishonors. Thus, I write from place of sincere empathy (identification, compassion, and understanding).

Abortion has the ability to wipe out posterity or our entire future generations. If you look around, who is there? When I got pregnant with my daughters, I chose not to be the last person standing in my bloodline – my seed would live. Abortion is being exalted and dressed in the guise of beauty and liberation; but the Holy Spirit said to me, "It is not a light matter." There is no beauty in abortion. Also, it is a dangerous choice to use as a normal practice of birth control. Accountability is associated with our choices.

This is *not* to criticize you; but to inform you. If you have had an abortion, or several, God still loves you! He sees you; He will forgive you and heal you of every emotional pain and mental trauma associated with abortion. Just ask Him; the answer is yes! Forgiveness is a gift and it is extended to all who want it. God will give you beauty for ashes – an exchange of your pain for His peace, your sorrow for His joy, and hope forevermore (Isaiah 61:1-3). Once you have asked and received God's forgiveness, forgive yourself and move forward.

Psalm 127:3 says, *"Behold, children are a heritage from the Lord, the fruit of the womb is a reward."* Children are a blessing from the Lord – His gift of life and love. It is God's will that children be conceived in the confinements of marriage. However, we know that often it does not happen this way. Even still, it does not change the fact that children are cherished gifts from God and you, mom, are a valuable manager in other people's lives (Psalm 127:3; Proverbs 29:17).

Sometimes, it can be tough raising children; however, I encourage you to pray to Father God, and ask for His wisdom on how to foster and relate with them. Even the grown ones, because relationships take on various forms and can require new ways of communicating. Families with both parents in the home or involved with their children, will still need divine counsel from the Lord. We do not have all the answers, but God does. And, it helps to have a friend or counselor who can supply encouragement and sound advice.

Think about this, we are all someone's child or daughter; and when we commit our lives to God, we become His daughters – children of God, the Father. Jesus gave His life for life, not death. Choose life; it is a beautiful reward! And, the God who sees you, will meet all of your needs according to His riches in glory (Philippians 4:19 AMP).

Chapter 11

REIGNING MIND

"And consider the example that Jesus, the Anointed One, has set before us. Let His mindset become your motivation." – Philippians 2:5 TPT

JESUS CHRIST IS OUR LIFE EXAMPLE; HE IS THE epitome of how we speak, think and act. What and how we think can either motivate or demotivate; it also influences our decisions, lifestyles, how we relate to people and how we view ourselves. These are some reasons why it is imperative to have the mind of Christ or have His perspective on living life.

For Christ's mindset to be operative in you, Jesus Christ must become your Lord and Savior. It is impossible to think like Him without, first, being His. Anyone can go through the motions or pretend; but God wants genuine godly attitudes that spring from real relationships with Him. Mindset is an established set of mental attitudes or a fixed state of mind, which affects our emotions, decisions, communication and outcome.

Right thinking is transformed thinking (Romans 12:2); and to be spiritual minded is life and peace (Romans

8:6). Our actions are the fruit of our thinking. Be aware and alert! Every thought we think is not from God. *"Don't become so well adjusted to your culture that you fit into it without even thinking"* (Romans 12:2a MSB). We need to have the mind of Christ so we can sift and reject thoughts and plans that are not in compliance with God's Word and will, and accept those that are. Jesus' mindset also connected with His speech – what He did or did not say; His thoughts and will were revealed through His choices and actions.

Jesus' mind was sound; irrespective of what He was challenged with or who He had to face, such as the apostate Pharisees and Sadducees, Caiaphas the high priest or Pontius Pilate. Consider the night before the crucifixion when Jesus was in the Garden of Gethsemane where He experienced spiritual, mental and emotional stress beyond human capacity. Yet, this did not cause Him to lose His mental and emotional stability and forfeit His purpose. Jesus did not bow to the magnitude of pressures by stopping or quitting; rather He bowed His will and entire being to the Father in prayer – the One who was always able to deliver (Hebrews 5:7-10). *"He prayed even more passionately, like one being sacrificed, until he was in such intense agony of spirit that his sweat became drops of blood, dripping onto the ground"* (Luke 22:44 TPT). Jesus' response to His approaching persecution was, *"But no matter what, your will must be mine"* (Luke 22:42b TPT).

Hardships come to us all and no one is exempt. Our roaring adversary is Satan and one of his main tactics is to produce fear in our hearts and minds – especially during times of adverse confrontations. Fear is a tormenting spirit that generates anxiety, doubt, unbelief and stress that can contribute to nervousness and other ailments. It produces images of the worse and not the best; it also activates thinking from a place of defeat and hopelessness, and not victory. Fear contributes to illogical thinking – thoughts that are inconsistent with God's Word and plans for you. Ungodly fear is always meant to harm you and hamper your calling and career.

In the backdrop of fiery persecution, Paul said to Timothy, *"For the Spirit God gave us does not make us timid, but gives us power, love and self-discipline"* (2 Timothy 1:7 NIV). Self-discipline or sound mind is having the ability to control one's thoughts, feelings, and emotions in the core of circumstances, regardless of its severity or weight of the concern. Mastery over the mind and heart, and responding by the Spirit of God, depicts sound judgement. Just like this Scripture states, this fear does not originate from God. Just as Jesus did, we have to press into God's Presence and from this union, the Spirit of God releases His power in us to stand up in the face of smashing situation. Holy Spirit imparts the ability to retain faith in soul-searing heart break, and forgive the offender. He gives us the stamina and resilience to go through as victors and finish the task. Holy Spirt imparts in us the grace to love anyhow. Even when it feels as though or we think we are going to break, we do not because of God's proficient power. Courage arises and cringing fear is powerless.

Having the mind of Christ is paramount for the Christian because it cultivates Holy Spirit inspired composure and leadership in life's complications. In both calm and commotion, we need Christ's perception. At times we may think that there is no solution to our problem specifically stated in the Word; however, when you seek and pray to Jesus, who is the Word, He will provide the answer. That which has been overshadowed with uncertainty will be made clear (Matthew 7:7 AMP).

When Jesus (Yeshua) becomes Master in our lives, our mind or thinking must be reeducated or renewed by the Word of God. Renewing our minds refer to a *new* way of thinking that aligns with the character and will of God and not the culture of worldliness. There is a clashing of the minds – Christ's mind and the world's. Romans 12:2 TPT instructs us to: *"Stop imitating the ideals and opinions of the culture around you, but be inwardly transformed by the Holy Spirit through a total reformation of how you think. This will empower you to discern God's will as you live a beautiful life satisfying and perfect in his eyes."*

How we think streams into every part of our life; so, we cannot allow any kind of thoughts to enter our minds unchecked. Some thoughts must not be permitted; if we do, we authorize that influence to dictate or direct us, which can give place to suffering, bondage, lost or unfulfilled purpose. Satan wars for our minds so he can have a place from which to rule; in view of this, it is absolutely mandatory to take every thought and purpose captive to the obedience of Christ (2 Corinthians 10:5). Having the mind of Christ is like having an impenetrable helmet on your head, known as the helmet of salvation (Ephesians 6:17). This helmet represents a mind filled with the knowledge and revelation of God's Word, and acts upon it, which will oppose and dethrone Satan's mental assaults and lies. Knowledge is power and Satan will use what he knows about you to subjugate you – even use Scripture to do it. Every thought out of alignment with God's Word must be taken captive, as a solider takes a prisoner captive with a spear in his back; otherwise, you will become the hostage of a stronghold. Faulty patterns of thinking can not be reasoned with; they must be scrutinized and subdued with the truth and authority of God's Word. Keep your shield of faith up so you can extinguish the flaming mind missiles of the enemy. He attempts to confuse your mind and cloud your purpose and identity. He offers enticing power and prestige, and desires you to act presumptuously and do things out of God's timing. Satan wants your worship; he wants your allegiance; he wants to be your master (Matthew 4:1-11).

Fear, deception and idolatry are typical satanic strongholds or iron grips. God's knowledge, His Word, releases overcoming power so that we will not be overcome, but remain overcomers in Christ and accomplish our callings and careers. Man's know-how and willpower is no match for Satan's cunningness. Decreeing the rhema Word of the Lord and Holy Spirit Empowerment have the capacity and might to take control of and rout demonic thoughts and forces. The blood of, and the name of Jesus (Yeshua) are imperative weapons of warfare to destroy demonically influenced thoughts. *"Wisdom brings strength and knowledge gives power"* (Proverbs 24:5 CEV). As we purposely continue to feed our minds God's Word, our spiritual and mental attitudes and decisions become Holy Spirit led and will prevent Satan from lodging a stronghold in our minds (2 Corinthians 10:3-5).

First Peter 1:13 charges us to gird up the loins of our minds; girding up the loins of your mind is the image of a person girding up his loins by tucking his long robe into the belt around his waist in order to run without hinderance. It has the meaning of being ready, prepared for action. An untucked robe would trip him up. Otherwise speaking, remove the loose, wrong thinking and grab ahold of those dangling thoughts that trip you up and prepare your mind and heart to obey God in every situation and at every moment.

A sound mind is a secure mind that is guarded, grounded and girded by the reigning power of God's Word. Your mind is crowned with the mind of Christ and the scepter is in your hand. God has given you the Holy Spirit of power to rule and reign in Christ our King!

Chapter 12

EMERGING DAUGHTERS

"For with God nothing is ever impossible and no word from God shall be without power or impossible of fulfillment." – Luke 1:37 AMPC

SARAH, REBEKAH (GENESIS 25:21), RACHEL (Genesis 29:31), Hannah (1 Samuel 1:2, 6), Elizabeth (Luke 1:7), and Manoah's wife (Judges 13:2) all had something in common – barrenness. It is remarkable that God used their infertility to demonstrate His omnipotence – unlimited, autonomous power. Absolutely nothing would prevent the God who makes things happen (Psalm 77:14 MSG), promises and plans from emerging. Job testified, *"I know that you can do all things, and that no purpose of yours can be thwarted"* (Job 42:2).

There is no darkness that God's power cannot penetrate. So, do not be intimidated by the dark places; God is Lord over it, and in the darkness too (Exodus 20:20-21). There is no problem too impossible that He cannot solve and no barrenness too sterile that God cannot cause you to conceive or be productive. There are seasons in our lives when it appears that nothing is happening, and the promises promised turn into ambiguity and faith is no longer standing still – faith is fading and fluctuating between the promise and the problem. Barrenness is an awful feeling of dryness – nothingness and unproductivity; it can seem as though God is nowhere to be found or He has withdrawn His Presence, and hope is vanishing.

Daughter of God take heart! God will dispel the darkness and lighten your way and remove the weight. Your problem is not a problem to God; nothing is too hard for Him (Jeremiah 32:27). Birthing contractions are excruciating, but when it is time to push you have to push even during the pain. Spiritually speaking, regardless of the pressure and pain, push! God spoke some promises long ago and it has yet to manifest; and the longevity of the promises are stretching, and it feels so uncomfortable and unbearable. Even still, trust God and push! Endurance is faith stretched out.

In natural pregnancy, the baby is hidden for nine months in the dark womb of the mother; as the baby grows and repositions his or herself, it becomes extremely uncomfortable and tight. Even the mother's skin grows to accommodate the enlarging of her abdomen and weight gain is natural. Nearing the conclusion of pregnancy, the mother can become anxious and unsettled to birth the child for reasons such as ready for her body to get back to normal and shed the weight, eliminate discomforts associated with pregnancy or excited to see, hold and lovingly care for her child.

Hannah had a heart-aching problem – barrenness. This was considered a curse during her time and associated with shame. Not only was she dealing with cultural perceptions, she was also dealing with constant commotion in her home

– Peninnah. Peninnah, Elkanah's second wife, intentionally thundered against Hannah with penetrating insults and berating comments about her barrenness. *"And her rival also provoked her severely, to make her miserable, because the Lord had closed her womb"* (1 Samuel 1:2, 6 NKJV). Perhaps Peninnah thought that she was in a more favorable position because she had children and Hannah had none. Her rival was a cruel enemy who frequently goaded her with pain staking remarks that caused her much sorrow, anger and tears (1 Samuel 1:7). More than likely they argued at times, but Peninnah's comments became overwhelming and what hurt even more was that her comments about Hannah's barrenness were true. Arguing with Peninnah would have been useless and could not produce the result that Hannah desired. The years of heartbreak and barrenness had taken a toll on her soul. *"And she was in bitterness of soul, and prayed to the Lord and wept in anguish"* (1 Samuel 1:10 NKJV). She focused on the problem so often that it is likely that she had mind battles wondering if God had rejected her. Yet, she resolved that only God could help her and fulfill her heart's cry. Deep calls unto deep; the depth of her need called to the depth of God's supply. Her emptiness pulled on the fullness of God (Psalm 42:7). So, she turned her face to the One that could break the stigma, the effects of the harsh statements, open her womb and give her a child – specifically a son (1 Samuel 1:11).

"And it happened, as she continued praying before the Lord (1 Samuel 1:12a). Her lips were moving; no voice was heard; yet, Hannah spoke loudly in her heart to the Lord. Eli observed Hannah's mouth moving and assumed she was intoxicated; He misunderstood her sorrow for drunkenness and rebuked and demanded her to put away her wine

(1 Samuel 1:13-15). Hannah replied, *"Count not thine handmaid for a daughter of Belial: for out of the abundance of my complaint and grief have I spoken hitherto"* (1 Samuel 1:16 KJV). She urged Eli not to think of her as a worthless, wicked woman – a surrogate for Satan – instead, a woman of a sorrowful spirit (1 Samuel 1:15). Heavily burden and deeply anguished, she humbly prayed and poured out of her soul to the Lord – not a cup of wine or strong drink to her mouth. She emptied her vexing cares and her heart's desires to the Lord of Hosts and vowed that if God would give her a son, she would dedicate him to the Lord for His service (1 Samuel 1:11). Hannah did not drink her problems away; instead, she abided for a lengthy time in the presence of the Lord where the fullness of her desires could be satisfied, and joy resides (Psalm 16:11). Eli realized that he had wrongly judged a broken and blameless daughter of God. *"Then Eli answered and said, 'Go in peace; and may the God of Israel grant your petition that you have asked of Him'"* (1 Samuel 1:17 AMP). Eli spoke words of peace to Hannah that took on a form of a prophetic pronouncement and prayer of agreement. *"When hope's dream seems to drag on and on, the delay can be depressing. But when at last your dream comes true, life's sweetness will satisfy soul"* (Proverbs 13:12 TPT). She pressed through in prayer and accepted Eli's words as assurance God would answer her prayers. No longer sad and afflicted, Hannah left in faith believing that her petition for a son had been answered.

"So it came to pass in the process of time Hannah conceived and bore a son, and called him Samuel, saying, 'Because I have asked for him from the Lord.'" (1 Samuel 1:20). Hannah was barren; but her prayer life was not. Prayer and her reliance on the Lord were channels of change and birthing. Hannah

did not revoke her vow to the Lord. She obediently gave back to the Lord what He had graciously given to her – Samuel. *"The Lord gave him to me and now I have returned him, whom I obtained by prayer, to the Lord as one asked or demanded"* (Unger's Commentary, OT, pg. 364). Samuel, born through the promise of God and prayer, became a mighty prophet and judge of Israel (1 Samuel 3; 7:15).

As it is in natural birth, there are similarities in spiritual birth; there is a process that we must undergo before the emerging of spiritual gifts and walking in the purposes that God have orchestrated for us to fulfill. In this process of development and waiting we can experience annoyance, anguish, tears and anger; and no matter how we may have temper tantrums and express our displeasure, it does not quicken the process nor does it eliminate it. There is no way to avoid it except by abandonment, which can result in terminating God's purposes. The Lord requires our cooperation (Philippians 2:13 AMPC). Jesus completely finished the work of His Father (John 4:34); and because the Finisher lives inside of you, you are a finisher too (Philippians 1:6).

Also in physical birth, the doctor provides the mother with care instructions that will help her and the baby to be and remain nutritionally fit and strong, such as eating a variety of foods that contain necessary nutrients, pre-natal vitamins, exercise, drink liquids as directed and keeping scheduled check-ups. Some prohibitions to avoid are smoking (or any harmful consumption), and before taking medicines, speak with your health care provider.

When God is birthing His purposes, there will always be some form of opposition – either satanic and/or the challenge of conquering the flesh. There are some things that are indispensable during the emerging process. *Emerge* means to arise, come on the scene, develop, come out, come into view, to cause to stand, erect, build, endure, to be fixed, to be valid, to be proven, to persist, stir up, to carry out, to become powerful (Strong's H6965).

I am reminded of a butterfly's cocoon; it is in that dark, tight place all by itself; yet it is a place of maturation and protection. This is enlightening because we tend to think only bad things happen in darkness. Babies develop and are shielded in the dark wombs of their mothers too. It is born with an innate awareness and ability to fly; but it knows that it cannot come out of the cocoon or shelter too soon; or else its potential and purpose would never be attained. It would not transform into the beautiful butterfly, get its wings, nor fly as God created it to do – its development would be deformed. The four stages of metamorphosis must be completed before it gets its wings and live out its purpose. Butterflies work to carry pollen from plant to plant, helping vegetables, fruits and flowers produce new seeds.

Before emerging there is a hiding; otherwise stated, it is spending much time with God alone in the secret place of spiritual union. After a time, this can begin to feel secluded and you may experience edginess; still it is important to remain focused and disciplined and not allow feelings to move you out the places of transition, progress and prayer. Nothing takes the place of prayer, not skill or know-how, if prayer lacks priority, your vital connection with God has been disrupted and fruitfulness will be stunted and incomplete (John 15:5 TPT). Prayer and God's Word are life-forces; you cannot live or produce properly without them; they are the life-flow of God's breath and Presence.

Prayer and the Word are standards of living for the woman of faith's existence. Furthermore, a constant emerging practice is building ourselves up on our most holy faith by Holy Spirit led prayers and praying in tongues (Jude 1:20). Praying in tongues rekindles passion, imparts restoration, and ushers us into different realms of the Spirit.

In the beginning was the Word and the Word, although being God, was face-to-face with God – the Father and Son (John 1:1-2). Prayer brings us up-close and personal with God; it brings us Face to face with Him, breath to breath – the Creator with His creation. Prayer is a place of encountering God's Presence.

It is compulsory to be insulated, cocooned in prayer and the Word until your process is completed. Your process is not for you alone; what God develops in you will be used to help transform and influence the lives of other people through the life-giving Spirit of God. We must lean into God so we can be fully empowered to proclaim the light and liberty of Christ, and release healing to the broken and bound, weary and wounded souls (Isaiah 61:1).

Separation is a part of emerging. God's Word tells us to come out from among them (2 Corinthians 6:17), and to lay aside encumbrances (Hebrews 12:1), which can hinder His plans from emerging in our lives. We have to be intentional about removing actions, attitudes and baggage that negatively affect our walk of faith and representation of the Lord. Let go of unforgiveness, jealousy, gossip, spitefulness, prejudice, competition, comparison, intoxication, and getting a buzz. Also, profanity is not pretty; they are ugly, foul words and are not a part of God's language. Cursing is not a mark of maturity nor sophistication. Whatever it is that prohibits your progress or keep tripping or entangling you, lay it aside (Colossians 3:8; Hebrews 12:1). Release the piercing wounds of the past and the present too. Many other people have experienced a lot, or even more tribulations than we have, and have overcome by God's grace and living victoriously. There is a cloud of biblical and contemporary examples of people who persisted in prayer (Luke 18:1), and pushed through the pressures and received the promise. Holy Spirit, the Spirit of power, is faithful and is ever present to help with those pestering matters so your potential can be fulfilled in Christ.

Another component of emerging is praise. If you do not praise God during the preparation, it can adversely affect your mind and emotions. Preparation does not always feel good. Nevertheless, praise is a gage that can direct and re-direct our focus. Praise has the capacity to lift burdens and give an accurate and fresh perspective; it can impart peace in an unsettled soul. More importantly, it focuses your heart, trust and appreciation on God's sovereignty, and releases the strength needed to continue and conquer. Prior to emerging, there is a proving ground of faithfulness, and praising and being thankful to God will help you endure the tests. Paul and Silas prayed and sang praises to God while in prison. The doors of the prison were opened and their chains fell off through a powerful earthquake. An audience of prisoners were listening to them from their cells as they worshipped God (Acts 16:25-27). Murmuring and complaining would not have produced the same results. There are realized and unrealized audiences who watch to see how you handle yourself during pressure, persecution and preparation. Undaunted, Paul and Silas prayed while in prison; and sung praise songs to the God of deliverance. Through their praise and prayers their hearts were raised into the joyous presence and peace of God, which provided a channel for God's power to manifest and operate in their circumstances. They could have escaped but did not; God had a greater purpose. After witnessing the display of God's might, the jailer asked Paul and Silas, *"What must I do to be saved?"* (Acts 16:30). After they explained eternal salvation, the jailer and his entire household accepted Jesus Christ as their Lord and personal Savior (Acts 16:31-34). God's purpose and plans for Believers will always include other people that do not personally know Him.

Praise changes the soul's climate. A thermometer fluctuates dependent upon the temperature. A soul controlled by the Spirit and God's Word will not be circumstance-controlled; but will praise God in spite of. Praise attracts God's presence; it enlists God's help during the preparation and in your situations. God inhabits the praise of *His* people (Psalm 22:3). In other words, God "dwells" in the atmosphere of praise. Praise is a vehicle of faith which brings us into the presence and power of God. If you are having difficulty trusting God, praise can ignite your faith and dispel doubt. *"God is wise and powerful! Praise him forever and ever"* (Daniel 2:20). Holy Spirit fuel is imparted when we praise God; new strength replaces fatigue and weakness, and fear is subjugated (Psalms 34:1; 59:17).

There is a process in natural birth called crowning; this is when the crown of the baby's head comes into view or begins to emerge. This step is the pushing stage of labor, which helps push the baby through the birth canal. The final stage concludes with the baby's delivery and placental expulsion; the afterbirth is no longer needed because birth of the new baby has arrived. Similarly, with our rebirth in Christ, the afterbirth of the old nature is removed and a new nature is born.

Regardless of where you are in your emergence process, there are steps of necessity that will lead to the full development of God's promises for your life. Trust God; He knows exactly what it takes.

It is exciting to hear personal prophecy pertaining to God's plans for ministry, spiritual gifts, businesses, property ownership, or how He wants to use you to make an impact for His glory. Prophetic words get the devil's attention. So, be alert to impending opposition. Remember, God's Word will never fail nor fade; so, it is vital that we declare the sayings of God – declare what God declared to you. Do not allow the opposition to cause you to feel or think that what God said will not come to pass.

I was given a personal prophecy about the next book that I write would be for women. I was challenged with procrastination and distractions, which were impeding my motivation and momentum. Even while writing this book, I felt edgy and hyperactive, which was working against me because I could not sit still long enough to write more than one or two paragraphs. I literally felt like I needed a hug from Jesus! For two days, I began thinking about who I could call for prayer to help me settle down and experience peace in my soul. It is a wise practice to ask the Lord who should pray for you, because everyone is not for you and do not want you to be successful. The feelings were strong; but I knew quitting was not an option and that I had to persist, pursue and prophesy. I sensed a stirring to pray aloud and prophesy the Word of the Lord. My prayer-thoughts transitioned from my mind to my mouth. The Lord of the breakthrough intervened and caused His peace to prevail in my soul. He released a fresh focus in order for me to accomplish His will. Afterwards, I picked up a calendar, without knowing this was written on it, *"My grace is always more than enough for you, and my power finds its full expression through your weakness"* (2 Corinthians 12:9 TPT). Amazing! This is the women's book that was prophesied!

Disenchantment can be a destiny blocker due to failed hopes, which can lead to a lack of joy. Be watchful not to allow dissatisfaction cause you to seek after other gods (idolatry), or practice divination, and turn you away from serving and worshipping the True and Living God. *"Do not turn to mediums [who pretend to consult the dead] or to spiritists [who have spirits of divination]; do not seek them out to be defiled by them. I am the Lord your God"* (Leviticus 19:31; Acts 16:16-18 AMP). Images and figurines of false deities (gods/goddess) are open doors for demonic activity (Psalm 115:1-9; Acts 19:19 AMP). These are abominable practices that the Lord detests.

Procrastination is a definite impediment to emerging! Habitual postponement is a thief of time and completion. There is a deceptiveness about delaying things because it excuses what we should be doing now. Proverbs 6:4 offers this counsel, *"Don't put it off, and don't rest until you get it done"* (TPT). Constantly saying what you are going to do, and not do it, is ineffective and does not help your dreams become reality – they remain in the dream realm. Not only does procrastination robe us of progress, it eliminates our peace because of not complying with the will of the Lord.

Our feelings have to be submitted to the Holy Spirit; because whether we feel like it or not, the task must be done. Only working when you feel like it, can be indicative of laziness, lack of drive, discipline and focus. We also have to guard against apathy and mediocrity. *"Whatever you do [whatever your task may be], work from the soul [that is, put in your very*

best effort], as [something done] for the Lord and not for men"
(Colossians 3:23 AMP). A word to the wise, walk by faith
and not by feelings. *"If you want to reign in life, don't sit on
your hands"* (Proverbs 12:24 TPT). Be devoted to God and
work diligently on your undertakings.

Even if you have impeded your pace or abandoned God's
call, arise! Emerge from that place of inaction and frustration;
hope in God; repent and get back on course. Repentance is a
canal for birthing; it is a route to reconciliation, restoration,
refocus and realization. Proclaim the Word of the Lord:

> *"The Lord God is my strength [my source of
> courage, my invincible army];*
>
> *He has made my feet [steady and sure] like
> hinds' feet*
>
> *And makes me walk [forward with spiritual
> confidence] on my*
>
> *high places [of challenge and responsibility]."*
>
> *Habakkuk 3:19 AMP*

High places or troubling times are commonly used by
God for our spiritual and mental fortitude, emotional maturity and equipping, which teaches us greater reliance on the
Lord that can result in increased anointings, abilities and
assignments. God is the One who gives the vision; so, the
only way to walk it out is with Him.

A hind is a female deer; she can place her hind feet or
hooves exactly where her front feet stepped, and be not

one inch off. In times of danger, she can run securely and stay on track. God's tests our faith to build us (James 1:2-4 AMP); Satan tempts to break us and cause our failure (1 Thessalonians 3:5 AMP); and whether you are being tested or tempted, stay on God's trajectory for your destiny. *"Look straight ahead, and fix your eyes on what lies before you. Mark out a straight path for your feet: then stick to the path and stay safe. Don't get sidetracked; keep your feet from following evil"* (Proverbs 4:27 NLT). Place your plans before God, get His affirmation, then proceed. *"Many plans are in a man's mind, but it is the Lord's purpose for him that will stand (be carried out)"* (Proverbs 19:21 AMP).

What was the Word that God spoke to you? It still stands; that Word is actively alive and will not be altered. God's Words are matchless and yields your potential and purpose! Anyone else's words that are contrary to who God says you are and what He said you will achieve, declare ineffective and inoperative in your life – regardless of who said it! God's Word is matchless and outweighs all verbal attacks. Some people are not going to believe God's plans for you, and will speak against it; what really matters is that you believe, and do it!

Daughter of power use your voice of distinction and significance to superimpose God's will in your life; realize that your voice is a conduit of redemptive and mountain-moving authority. You are a part of a legislative assembly, a governing authority – the *ekklesia*. You are anointed with creative capacity and have been given life-changing capabilities. Daughter of the Kingdom, you are smeared with the Holy Spirit's Presence to achieve unprecedented things for God's glory (Isaiah 43:19)!

Selected one, in whom God delights in demonstrating and revealing Himself as I AM, you are loved by Him. This love is extraordinary and has the superpower to burst through any barrier, regardless of its magnitude. By the Lord's mighty hand, you will triumph and accomplish just what God said that you will! Woman, emerge!

> *"And I pray that he would unveil within you the unlimited riches of his glory and favor until supernatural strength floods your innermost being with his divine might and explosive power"* (Ephesians 4:16 TPT).

> *"Never doubt God's mighty power to work in you and accomplish all this. He will achieve infinitely more than your greatest request, your most unbelievable dream, and exceed your wildest imagination! He will outdo them all, for his miraculous power constantly energizes you"* (Ephesians 4:20 TPT).

Chapter 13

REIGNING WORDS
PRAYER OF SALVATION

*"For it is by grace[God's remarkable compassion
and favor drawing you to Christ] that you have
been saved [actually delivered from judgment
and given eternal life] through faith. And this
[salvation] is not of yourselves [not through your
own effort], but it is the [undeserved gracious]
gift of God; not as a result of [your] own works
[nor your attempts to keep the Law], so that no
one will [be able to] boast or take credit in any
way [for his salvation]."* – Ephesians 2:8-9 AMP

FATHER GOD, IN THE NAME OF JESUS, I ASK YOU
to forgive me of all my sins and transgressions.
Liberate me from every behavioral bent of iniq-
uity; and cleanse me from all unrighteousness. Father, I
confess the truth of Your Word and believe in my heart
that Jesus Christ is Lord! Thank You for raising Your Son
from the dead; because without this great miracle, my
salvation would be impossible. God, thank You for Your

unconditional love and peace, and for welcoming me into Your family.

Lord, now that I am saved, let it be according to Your Word, *"baptize and empower me with the Holy Spirit,"* so that I will be enabled to live victoriously and be equipped for Kingdom service. In Jesus' name, amen!

> *"In this new creation life,*
>
> *your nationality makes no difference, or your ethnicity, education,*
>
> *or economic status – they matter nothing.*
>
> *For it is Christ that means everything as he lives in every one of us!" (Colossians 3:11 TPT).*

BREAKTHROUGH PRAYER OF FAITH

Jesus replied, "Have faith in God [constantly]." I assure you and most solemnly say to you, whoever says to this mountain, 'Be lifted up and thrown into the sea!' and does not doubt in his heart [in God unlimited power], but believes that what he says is going to take place, it will be done for him [in accordance with God's will]." – Mark 11:22-23 AMP

A MOUNTAIN IS EMBLEMATIC OF AN OBSTRUCtion, limitation or an insurmountable complication. "Mountain-remover" was a name associated with wise or good teachers who had the ability to remove the difficulties of understanding in the minds of their intellectuals. Unflinching faith and prevailing prayer are tools of victory that will help us to conquer difficulties as well as endure them.

Father, in the name of Jesus Christ, I intercede for the readers of this book. I am convinced that You can do anything, and that no opposition is too powerful to withstand Your power. Lord, You are sovereign and everything is subject to Your Word! So, I ask You to release the rhema Word that she needs in order to succeed!

Uproot unforgiveness and attitudes that are inconsistent with Your holy character and cultivate the fruit of the Spirit within her. Expunge old, debilitating mind-sets; erase and heal the pains and hauntings of her past, and empower her to arise and walk in the newness of life in Christ Jesus! Lord, dislodge fear and release boldness and relentless faith; replace brokenness with wholeness; uproot defeat and impart victory! Let truth prevail that will dispel all manners of deception.

Jesus, Your Word declares that You are Baal-perazim, the Master of breakthroughs; and there is absolutely no demonic stronghold or struggle that exists that can hinder Your delivering power! Let every satanic plot against her be destroyed by the hammer of Your Word! Lord, I declare the decree that Your Word is fruitful, and on a divine mission to produce prosperity and fruition of purpose in her life (Isaiah 55:11)! Remove every limitation and release the anointing of the Breaker to burst her out of every harmful mental, emotional, physical, financial and spiritual enclosure. Annihilate every yoke of enslavement and reverse every decision made for her demise.

Holy Spirit, loose Your mighty power like a furious rushing river to drive out her enemies! I rebuke every destiny destroyer and demonically driven distraction; and declare the manifestation of unbroken focus and determination.

By the might and power of the Holy Ghost, you will slay every satanic Goliath and walk in the revelation of the blood covenant of Jesus Christ!

Father, release fresh winds and fires of Your Spirit that will ignite her to continually triumph and reign in Jesus' name! Amen!

FAITH DECLARATION & AFFIRMATION

"It is through him that we live and function and have our identity; just as your own poets have said, 'Our lineage comes from Him" – Acts 17:28 TPT

In the authority of God's Word,
I decree and declare that I am a WOW Woman –
a woman submitted and committed to the Lordship of
Jesus Christ.
I am washed and purified by the blood of the
Lamb of God.
I am a vessel of righteousness, victory and Holy
Spirit power.
I am like a tree planted by the rivers of living water.
I bring forth fruit in its season; and all that
I do shall prosper because my plans are approved by You.
I am healed, made whole and bold as a lion.
I am favored, beautiful and blessed.
I am worthy, wanted and loved by my Father – God.
Jesus Christ occupies preeminence in my life;
therefore, I prevail and excel.
I am a mountain mover, a chain breaker and a
covenant-keeper.

I am anointed by the Most High.
My prayers are powerful and effective.
My worship is in spirit and in truth.
God's Word is the compass in my life.
I slay every destiny destroyer and rebuke
the spirits of sabotage, python and rejection.
I am no longer constrained, God's
power has set me free.
I rebuke the spirit of fear; it is not my friend.
Faith is my companion and door-opening key.
I walk in the spirit of power, love and a sound mind.
I am more than a conqueror through Christ.
He empowers me to win!
Behold, God has given me His authority and power to
trample upon serpents, scorpions and over all the power
of the enemy (Satan), and no harm shall befall me!
I rule and reign in Christ; therefore, I have the grace
capacity to decree a thing and it shall be established.
No weapon formed against me shall prosper.
For the Lord is my Shield and Buckler; He is the Rock
of my salvation, my strong Deliverer and High Tower!
The Lord is my Shepherd and He leads me on the paths of
success and safety. I shall not be moved. I capture, like
prisoners of war, all demonically inspired thoughts and
command that they bow to Jesus Christ. I have the mind
of the Anointed One!
The Lord is for me. He is my Hero and Banner;
my Blueprint for victorious living!
I am a anointed to finish, and created for good works.
I will fulfill God's designed purpose and destiny!
In Jesus' name, Amen!

Poetry

THE SHE THAT YOU ARE MEANT TO BE

"We have become his poetry, a re-created people that will fulfill the destiny he has given each of us, for we are joined to Jesus, the Anointed One. God planned in advance our destiny and the good works we would do to fulfill it!"
- Ephesians 2:10 TPT

Blow the trumpet in Zion, sound an alarm, send up a flair.

Cry, shout, and holler – "WAKE UP!" you spiritually dead and hearing impaired. This is a universal call ladies, to mothers, daughters, and sisters everywhere.

Do you drink or smoke trying to stop up your ears, to silence the negative voices that you hear?

Are God's words being silenced by the enemy's cry, telling you that your destiny will never come before you die?

Is your time given solely to material gain, intellect, and your outward appearance?

Have you sown to the Spirit to reap life everlasting, or is your treasure in earthly inheritance?

Did the enemy find a seat through the words that you say, or gossip that you have rehearsed?

Causing your prayers to bounce off walls, and you to be bound, and yoked to generational curses?

Are you this SHE?..

That momma said was not pretty, or daddy left to early, or rape found you in your innocence?

Whose face is everchanging, emotions always showing, especially for those you think aren't listening?

Has your insides been stained with pains that remain, hurts that pervert, and secrets that have weakened you?

Have your hopes been derailed, and your dreams disappeared?

Well, dear sister, it's time for a breakthrough.

It is time to gird up the loins of your mind, and let soberness take control.

Cause this is the ultimate fight of your life, Satan wants to take your very soul.

It is time to say, "Search me Lord, remove all the masks and help me drop all my excuses."

Pull back the layers that hide the true you, drop the facades and expose all the abuses.

It is time for God to break the chains that keep you in pain, and bound to lies and untruths.

It is time to show this SHE inside of you, what's masking your sight, preventing God's truth to come through.

It is time for you to walk in power and authority, over tainted perceptions and polluted views.

It is time for Christ to set this SHE free, and *let the spirit of her mind be renewed.*

It is time for God to expose the enemy's disguise and cause your spiritual eyes to see.

Cause when God reveals the truth my sister, *it is the truth that shall make you free.*

How big is the universe?

How many stars are in the galaxy?

What is Einstein theory of relativity?

I have no idea!

But I know that it is this SHE that Christ will come to claim, on that day that He makes up His jewels.

And her likeness will be in the heavens, crowned with 12 stars, representing the 12 tribes that He rules.

She is a reflection of God's magnificence—beautiful, skillful, delicate and refined.

This she is made up of diversities and complexities that can virtually blow a man's mind.

Look at the stars they are uncountable, the number of sand untraceable, yet,

He knows the number of hairs and the destiny that this SHE seeks.

God made her a crown to her husband and a blessing to her children.

When she *openeth* her mouth with wisdom, it is this SHE that can bring men peace.

Let's go back to the opening bars of life, to the time when God said, *"Let there be!"*

Where *in the beginning was the Word, and Word was with God*, and *darkness was upon the face of the deep.*

The first man, he was formed, gathered from the dust of the ground,

from God's likeness and His image, and the breath of life as His crown.

And this SHE was created, draped in her femininity like a gown; and with this SHE creation was finished, and the Trinity sat down.

Yes, this SHE was the first woman that the world had ever known, brought to the man his plus one, when God said man should not be alone.

Now, I know Eve gave Adam the forbidden fruit to consume; but, no one seems to remember that she carried the first womb.

Nor, do they recall that through her was the miracle of childbirth, or that God used her to bring forth the Savior to the earth.

Like you and me they remember her past, writing it down and always keeping score, never considering that Seth was hers, and from his seed, *began men to call upon the name of the Lord.*

Yes, Abigail was wise, Ruth was faithful, and Esther I am told was fearless, but they each had a past to change, and thank God for His forgiveness.

So, when the enemy tells you something negative or fills your head with untruths, tell him about God's thoughts towards you, and how God named the church after you.

Let him know that you are *fearfully and wonderfully made*, rehearse the words out loud; let it echo in your ears, until no demon in hell can cause your mind to be swayed.

Remember ye not the former things, neither consider the things of old, let God do a new thing in you; let Him heal and renew your soul.

Bow your heads, close your eyes, and declare over your past its last will and testament.

Call, "Ashes to ashes and dust to dust!" cry and snot until every demon evacuates your residence.

Agree with God and decree that, *No weapon formed against* you *will prosper*!"

Throw your white flower upon the casket, and shed your last drops of tears, let the love of God transform you and heal the pain from your childhood.

So, I repeat my call to you again, "WAKE UP!" to those asleep and spiritually unresponsive.

To all races, ages, and social classes, to the atheist, and the new aged conscious.

I declare life and prosperity to this SHE, present in women everywhere; know that God has created you to be free, absent of bondage–chains or snares.

Do you know the thoughts that He thinks toward you, that they are of *peace, and not of evil?*

He will make your life shine like a star, and you to soar as an eagle.

Take on the Word of God, and let it come alive in you today.

It is *quick and powerful*, ensuring that you never go astray.

Determine to reject rejection, in whatever form you may encounter it.

Live, love and know your value; be an original – never a counterfeit.

Submit yourself to Him, open your heart and lend God your ears.

Know that you were created intentionally, drop all the walls and let go of all your fears.

Walk with integrity; let your light shine that others may see.

Allow God's hand to mend and mold you into **the SHE that you are meant to be**.

Poetry written by: Min. Dana Thomas
A New Leaf on Life Ministries, Inc.
Scripture text (KJV) has been italicized.

CPSIA information can be obtained
at www.ICGtesting.com
Printed in the USA
LVHW011555301120
673037LV00026B/5213